The Bleak Age

THE BLEAK AGE

J. L. HAMMOND

and

BARBARA HAMMOND

The Bleak Age

LONGMANS, GREEN AND CO.
LONDON · NEW YORK · TORONTO

THE BLEAK AGE

Based on " The Age of the Chartists "

BY

J. L. HAMMOND
Hon. D.Litt. Oxon.

AND

BARBARA HAMMOND
Hon. D.Litt. Oxon.

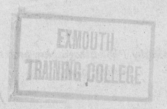

LONGMANS, GREEN AND CO.
LONDON ● NEW YORK ● TORONTO

LONGMANS, GREEN AND CO. LTD.
OF PATERNOSTER ROW
43 ALBERT DRIVE, LONDON, S.W.19
NICOL ROAD, BOMBAY
17 CHITTARANJAN AVENUE, CALCUTTA
36A MOUNT ROAD, MADRAS

LONGMANS, GREEN AND CO.
55 FIFTH AVENUE, NEW YORK

LONGMANS, GREEN AND CO.
215 VICTORIA STREET, TORONTO

Reprinted by Photolithographic process
January 1945

CODE NUMBER 11294

PREFACE

THE writers published in 1930, with the title *The Age of the Chartists*, a study of the social life of England in the thirties and forties of last century, giving special attention to the range and the character of the popular discontent that distinguished those years. In this little volume they have reconstructed and revised part of that book, in order to put into compact form the chapters that seemed to have a special bearing on our modern problem. For no problem to-day is more urgent than the problem that arises with the growth of leisure and the spread of common enjoyment. At first sight it may seem paradoxical to suggest that the way to examine the problems of an age of leisure is to study the experience of an age without leisure. Yet a little reflection will show that there is a vital connection between the two.

In the society described in the following pages the lot of the great mass of mankind was supposed to be the routine of eating, drinking, working, and sleeping. Leisure was the privilege of the few. The few therefore were educated to enjoy and use leisure; the mass of the population were educated for work, and for work that did not demand any considerable intelligence. Thus, for the general population, reason and feeling were left at the lowest level. Standards of taste and culture were in the keeping of a small class which had inherited, with leisure, the æsthetic and literary sensibilities that had been developed by generations accustomed to an atmosphere of ease and elegance. The Chartist movement, if the argument of this book is correct, was the revolt of the mass of the population against the bleak conditions to which this view of society reduced them. They refused to think of their own lives as nothing more than eating, drinking, working and sleeping.

It is difficult to imagine a greater contrast than the contrast between that age and our own. Leisure is no longer the privilege of the few. The diversions of leisure are now enjoyed by all classes, for mass production, first used to supply man's needs, is now used to supply his pleasures. The columns of our newspapers, the scenes at a Test Match, the crowded cinemas, the radio talking, singing, or acting, in every street, these, the chief phenomena of our social life, will give to posterity the impression of a society with universal leisure, depending no longer on the taste or judgment of the few for its guidance, but using universal suffrage in its manners as in its politics, in the choice of its culture as in the choice of its Parliaments. Of the revolutions that have followed the war this may prove to be the most important.

The importance of this change has not received the attention it deserves. Rostovtzeff, the social historian of the Roman Empire, discussing the decay that set in in the third century, asks a disconcerting question: "Is not every civilization bound to decay as soon as it begins to penetrate the masses?" His conclusion will seem unnecessarily gloomy to most people, but his question serves a useful purpose in reminding us that the new conditions under which we live offer a challenge to our civilization. The inventions that spread leisure have been followed by the inventions that provide everybody

with ways of using that leisure. It has often been said
of the steam-engine that it came into the world before
the world was ready for it. Future ages may make the
same comment on the cinema and the radio. For, if
they bring unprecedented opportunities for educating
reason and feeling, they bring unprecedented opportunities for corrupting them. Of these inventions it is even
truer than it was of the others, that their best use
demands the intelligent co-operation of the entire community. In the long run the test of our civilization will
be its success in producing a society that can choose
between the good use of these inventions and the bad.

Our chief danger comes from the tradition described
in this little volume. For though we have abandoned
the view that only a small class should have leisure, we
have not abandoned the implications that belonged to
it. We have not yet realized that our experiment—an
experiment new to history in respect of its scale—can
only succeed if we educate all classes for leisure. It is
absurd to expect from a raw mass of untrained mind and
emotion, submitted to the influences of the cinema and
the radio, an educated taste. The educated man can
respond to the stimulus of ideas or the beauty of art; the
uneducated man responds to effects that are sensational,
immediate, astonishing, and crude. And as the provision
of amusement is governed largely, though fortunately not
wholly, by commercial motives, the taste of the uneducated man is more likely to be satisfied than the more
exacting taste of the educated. The first effect of the
cinema has been the depression of the theatre just when
serious drama had made a remarkable recovery after a
century's eclipse. It is difficult to imagine the plays of
Euripides succeeding in a society where the entertainment of the theatre was organized and produced by

profit-making companies, for a society to whom leisure
was a new experience.

All this is so plain that the reader may retort that he
need not study the time of the Chartists to appreciate its
truth. Unfortunately we have not yet taken this truth
so seriously as to act upon it. We depend for the dis-
crimination between the good and the bad in our theatre,
our cinema, our literature, our press, on the judgment
of a society that is still brought up on the plan that was
in force when the mass of men and women were supposed
to have nothing to do with culture. It is true that we
spend large sums on popular education, and that we
provide large facilities for taking intelligent boys from
the poorest home to the University. But it is also true
that though everybody votes at twenty-one and that most
people begin to influence public taste long before twenty-
one, most boys and girls have no education after fourteen.
Yet there is surely no time when education is more
needed. For most purposes this population is an adult
population; it has passed into the world of industry; it
has a new sense of independence; it reads the newspapers;
goes to the cinema; listens to the wireless; chooses between
one pleasure and another; between a pleasure that merely
excites and a pleasure that enlarges the mind. In this
critical time when it is interpreting a new world, when
its mind and taste are being formed by all the influences
to which it is subject, when, owing to the perfection of
our machines it has adult habits without adult tasks, it
is deprived of all the education that the class educated
for leisure receives from literature or history, and is told
to trust to the school of life, a school in which, as beauty
and peace are steadily destroyed, few of its scholars can
hope to learn the wisdom that nature has taught mankind. Nearly twenty years ago Mr. Fisher provided a

plan to meet this urgent need. The need was urgent then; it is still more urgent now. Yet we are told that we cannot afford such a plan. This is only another way of saying that we think that a society can use leisure without being educated for it.

The challenge that is offered to us is offered of course to other societies of our time. But there is one respect in which we are trying to do something more ambitious than certain of our neighbours. In every society there is a mass mind that can be interested and excited by ideas and emotions. In the Chartist time England left this mind alone, giving scarcely any education and trusting to its police to prevent any dangerous outburst. In certain States to-day, Russia, Germany, Italy, a deliberate attempt is made to take this primitive force and to direct and control it, as the rulers of the State wish, making it a defence for a particular type of government. If we wanted to describe the ideal of our democracy, we should say that it attempts so to educate its citizens as to give them independent qualities of intelligence and temper, seeking a unity that is not merely the unity of the closed mind. It is a noble aim, but how do we set about it? We set about it as if we were still in the state of mind of the rulers of the age of the Chartists. For we treat as if they were still merely the servants of profit-making industry the mass of boys and girls between fourteen and eighteen who are to be the guardians of our culture.

HEMEL HEMPSTED,
    August 1934.

CONTENTS

CONTENTS

THE BLEAK AGE

CHAPTER I

INTRODUCTORY

DISCONTENT

IF anyone were asked to give the causes of the Gordon Riots he would not hesitate long about his answer. He might turn to the pages of *Barnaby Rudge* for a graphic picture of the nightmares that religious terror could excite in an ignorant and credulous populace. He might quote the letter in which Burke, who had risked his life in the riots, appealed to the Government to be moderate in the hour of punishment, on the ground that the guilt of the rioters was shared by the nation, since the law till lately had lent its sanction to intolerance, and the heads of the Church and Dissenting communities had wilfully encouraged it. He might describe the scene in a street in Newgate where a chimney-sweeper held a Bible upside down as he pretended to read it, while a mob searched the house of a trembling merchant. He would point to the weakness of a discredited Government, to the negligence of the City magistrates, to the want of a police force, in order to explain how lawlessness gained the

upper hand and London fell for some days into the wild
power of rage and plunder.

> " When the rude rabble's watchword was ' destroy '
> And blazing London seem'd a second Troy."

If the same person were asked to give the causes of the
Chartist movement, he would be much less ready with an
explanation. For he would see at once that no such
simple analysis would account for the facts; that this
agitation was connected with others, each of them significant of active and conscious discontent; that violence, the
most important fact in the Gordon Riots, was the least
important fact in the Chartist demonstrations; that un-
like the mob, drawn by a strong passion which spent
its inarticulate fury in burning Newgate prison to the
ground, the men and women who kept the Chartist movement alive had a steady and responsible quarrel with the
conditions of their lives, which gave a unity to efforts that
look distracted and confused. The London mob shout-
ing for Wilkes, for Gordon, for Queen Caroline, obeyed a
simple emotion; the silent crowds tramping to Newcastle
Moor or leaving the factories of Bradford or Halifax to
climb the overlooking hills for a Chartist meeting, obeyed
a deeper and more complex sense of wrong.

There was a good deal of lawlessness in eighteenth-
century England; particular grievances, like Enclosure
Bills, or dear food, or new machines, excited riots in one
place or another. This kind of violence continued in the
next century: the riots against the raising of prices for
the Covent Garden Theatre lasted several days, and
succeeded in their object; there were savage attacks on
the Irish quarter in more than one Northern town; in
1816 mobs were moving about in East Anglia with
banners inscribed " Bread or blood "; the enclosure of

Otmoor provoked small farmers and labourers to a kind of guerrilla struggle. But anyone who throws his mind over the succession of popular movements on a larger and less local scale in the nineteenth century will see that working-class discontent assumed in that century a more serious character and significance. The Luddite rising in the Midlands and the North in 1811 and 1812; the agrarian revolt in the southern counties in 1830; the passionate movement inspired by Owen which collected the energy and enthusiasm of the working classes throughout England for a great constructive idea in 1833; the Chartist agitation, in its several forms in the thirties and forties—all these are expressions of a spirit of which there is little trace in eighteenth-century England: the resentment of men convinced that there is something false and degrading in the arrangement and the justice of their world.

When this discontent appeared, sensible and public-spirited writers pointed out to the poor that they were much better off than their fathers and grandfathers. Invention had made commodities cheaper; food and clothing were more abundant; the mills increased family incomes; the poorest people wore stockings; and in other respects the humblest person enjoyed advantages that had been out of the reach of the lords and squires of other ages. These contentions have been repeated by recent writers who think that historians have been apt to draw the life of this time in colours too sombre for the truth. Statisticians tell us that when they have put in order such data as they can find, they are satisfied that earnings increased and that most men and women were less poor when this discontent was loud and active than they were when the eighteenth century was beginning to grow old in a silence like that of autumn. The evidence, of course, is scanty,

and its interpretation not too simple, but this general
view is probably more or less correct. If, then, there is
for the first time systematic and widespread discontent,
the explanation must be sought outside the sphere of
strictly economic conditions. The rebels, though they
included men and women who found it difficult to keep
the wolf from the door, were not composed altogether of
starving handloom weavers, or unemployed mill-workers.
There were other elements in the anger and the envy of
the times, and to understand what those elements were
it is necessary to look a little more closely into the
character of this new society and the general colour of
its life.

It is obvious that when men are wandering over the
steppes in search of food their pursuits and interests are
too narrow in range to make the term civilization suitable
to describe their manner of life. Civilization implies
some degree of independence; it implies that man has
learnt how to mould his surroundings to his own purposes; that he is not in complete subjection to nature or
even just holding his own in a stern struggle. If, then,
we are comparing the life of Manchester with the life of
the steppes or the tropical forest, we think chiefly of this
difference in material power. That is the distinguishing
difference. But when we compare two ages or two
societies, both of them in a later stage of development,
both of them able to follow a settled life and to express
their character, their tastes, and ideas in complicated and
deliberate institutions, we do not merely compare their
material circumstances. If we compare Western civilization with that of China, or the civilization of modern
Lancashire with that of Rome under Augustus, we do not
merely count the material advantages that one possesses
and the other lacks—railways, cotton mills, a stock

exchange, other signs and products of economic wealth. We survey the whole of their social life, their religion, their art, their literature, their methods of government and justice, the several institutions in which their public life finds form and expression, the relationships and the sentiments of classes to each other. We recognize, that is, that such a society has to satisfy a wider range of needs than the needs that the nomad is trying to satisfy on the steppes or the tropical man in the depths of the forest. To understand discontent we must keep this range in mind.

For discontent comes from the imagination. " Human sorrow springeth of man's thought." Poverty may produce such a state of the imagination; injustice may produce it; inequality may produce it; but we may find a society enduring great poverty, suffering what seems to us gross injustice, living under conditions so unequal as to look as if they were deliberately designed to provoke envy, in which discontent is unknown. We know that some men like St. Francis find happiness in poverty just because their imagination finds in renunciation and hardship a field for the sublime in thought and action. Bridges describes such natures in the *Testament of Beauty*

" And mystic Vision may so wholly absorb a man
   that he wil loathe ev'n pleasure, mortifying the flesh
   by disciplin of discomfort so to strengthen his faith.
   Thus tho' 'twas otherwise than on Plato's ladder
   that Francis climb'd—rather his gentle soul had learn'd
   from taste of vanity and by malease of the flesh—
   he abjured as worthless ev'n what good men will call good,"

To thinkers who held, as most Radicals held a century ago, that justice demanded that every adult man should have a vote for Parliament and that any other political arrangement was vicious, it seemed difficult to believe

that social life had been happy or successful when government had been despotism, despotism it may be with a
kind face, but still despotism. Yet as we look back over
history we see that almost every sort of government has
been made tolerable to human nature, and that men
and women have lived with equanimity under political
systems which left them not merely without political
rights, but without any pretence of personal liberty. In
such cases it is clear that in some way or by some device
these excluded men and women were given the sense of
sharing in the life of this society; their imagination and
their emotions were satisfied, some would say deceived,
by its dispositions or its illusions. For if men and women
are to be attached to a society, they must look on it as
something in which they have a part; a world in which
what we may call the common mind finds in some degree,
or by some means, scope, peace, comfort, and self-respect;
in which distinctions of class and fortune, however hardly
and sternly drawn, do not forbid all ties of sympathy, all
unity of sentiment.

Professor Graham Wallas, describing the difference
between the reactions produced by human and non-
human obstruction to our impulses, points out that when
Shakespeare sets out the ills that drive men to suicide he
gives

> " The oppressor's wrong, the proud man's contumely,
> The pangs of despised love, the law's delay,
> The insolence of office, and the spurns
> That patient merit of the unworthy takes,"

and does not mention the want of food and clothing from
which he must himself have suffered during his first
wanderings from Stratford. So Wordsworth draws a poor
man holding dispute

" With his own mind, unable to subdue
Impatience through inaptness to perceive
General distress in his particular lot;
Or cherishing resentment, or in vain
Struggling against it; with a soul perplexed,
And finding in herself no steady power
To draw the line of comfort that divides
Calamity, the chastisement of Heaven,
From the injustice of our brother man."

Neither Shakespeare nor Wordsworth would have doubted that a man might be less poor and less uncomfortable than his grandfather, and yet have in his consciousness a more wounding sense of baulked instincts, more of the sting of defeat, more of that impatience of calamity which springs from a belief that it is injustice. It is the aim of these pages to inquire what it was in the conditions and setting of English social life in the first half of the nineteenth century that created this sense of wrong.

CHAPTER II

THE REMEDY OF THE ANCIENT WORLD

COMMON ENJOYMENT

THE art of government may be described in one aspect as the art of making men and women think that the world they inhabit obeys in some degree their own ideas of justice. Cavour's often-quoted saying that anyone can govern in a state of siege meant, of course, that when you are released from this task and government becomes naked force, statesmanship, a rare quality, ceases to be needed, and firmness, which is more common, takes its place. Peoples, great and small, have often been ruled against their will by firmness. But clearly, if we wish to understand the discontent of the nineteenth century, we shall learn less from ages and places where government was of this character than from those in which rulers sought to justify their authority, and societies sought to satisfy their self-respect. Bacon pointed out that when Virgil attributed to Augustus the best of human honours he made this the mark of his rule:

> " Victorque volentes
> Per populos dat jura."

Bacon used this verse to illustrate his argument that " it was ever holden that honours in free monarchies and commonwealths had a sweetness more than in tyrannies, because the commandment extendeth more over the wills of men, and not only over their deeds and services." It may help us to understand the discontent of Manchester amid all the improvements and new knowledge that the Industrial Revolution brought, if we ask ourselves in what sense Virgil's boast was true, and what there was in Roman civilization which gave it the appearance of a voluntary or consenting society.

As we look back over the history of Graeco-Roman civilization we find every variety of political government, but through all those varieties we see that a definite effort was made to command the wills of men, and not merely their deeds and services. Elaborate care was taken to produce a stable society creating a sense of fellowship, by satisfying the imagination of the ruled, whether their political rights were considerable or insignificant. And as that civilization reflects the experience of the most capable peoples in Europe, whose society endured over a long space of time, it is worth while to consider what methods were used to make men and women think that the world in which they lived obeyed their own ideas of justice.

On this aspect of ancient history we have learnt a great deal in recent years from the discovery and interpretation of inscriptions. We see that what was most important in the civilization of classical Greece or the Hellenized East or the Roman Empire was the quality of its city life; the character of the institutions and customs which inspired or sought to inspire a common pride and common emotion in populations tempted into strife by savage inequalities of fortune and sharp antipathies of history and race. To appreciate the importance of those institutions it is necessary to remember what difficulties these societies had to overcome.

The struggles of rich and poor in ancient Greece, of city and city, were bitter and incessant. Greek literature is full of this strife; the fear of revolution is constant; Isocrates said that Greeks feared their fellow-citizens more than they feared a foreign enemy. The reason is partly that the Greeks were intelligent and contentious above their neighbours, pursuing ambitions greater and nobler (it has been said by Dr. Bevan that their great achievement was bringing freedom and civilization into union), partly that they lived in an atmosphere of fierce economic competition, and trade routes and commercial openings had an exceptional importance for peoples whose livelihood depended upon them.

It is not surprising, then, that Greek history is full of strife, and that it seems to end in political failure. Yet the history of the world has been largely moulded by the achievements of this small and distracted people: the new spirit they brought into politics; the beauty of art, life, and manners that fascinated first Macedon, then Rome; the literature and science that made them the teachers of Europe until the Roman Empire was lost in the Dark Ages, and again so soon as the Renaissance summoned the ghost of Greece from libraries and monasteries, where it had slept through the storm. A people apparently given up to war and conflict left these riches to mankind. What is the explanation? It is to be found in the power of disinterested emotion to lighten the dark misery that man suffers when shut up within the narrow circle of selfish aims and cares. The class struggle was veiled or softened by the moral influence of common possessions, the practice of social fellowship was stimulated by the spectacle of beautiful buildings, and the common enjoyment of the arts and culture of the time. If the many and the few, the rich and poor, had pursued their quarrels in a world untouched by this gentle and mysterious spirit, a State like Athens could not have lived long enough to lay her spell upon the world.

When we turn to the history of the East under Alexander's successors, we come on perpetual wars in which brothers contend with brothers and every king has a rival of his own blood, so that these rulers, proud as they were of their civilized traditions, seem to differ little in fact from the oriental despots whose culture they despised. Of the poverty and hardships of life among their subjects scholars like Dr. Tarn draw a melancholy picture. In the island of Rhodes, which takes the place of Athens as a pioneer, elaborate provision was made for the relief of the poor, but over most of the Hellenized East the poor were becoming poorer as prices rose and wages fell. There was all the material for revolution, and Naxos and other islands were the scenes of violent class struggles. The treaties made between Alexander and the states of the League of Corinth in 335 B.C. had contained some significant provisions. Both sides agreed to take precautions to prevent any state from proceeding to the confiscation of personal property, the division of land, the cancellation of debt, or the liberation of slaves for the purposes of revolution. The same kind of Holy Alliance reappears in Demetrius's League in 303 B.C. In the third century there was a revolution in Sparta described by Dr. Tarn which only failed because Cleomenes, who organized it and carried it at first to success, mixed plans for foreign conquest with his social schemes. Yet we find in the midst of all this strife of class and of fratricidal war between rivals for Alexander's empire, a brilliant city life, where the arts flourish and beauty and grace are admired. The Seleucid kings made deliberate efforts to foster and develop that life as the means to progress and unity, as an educating influence over the indigenous races brought into contact with Greek ideas. The saying that Arrian put into the mouth of Alexander (quoted by J. S. Reid in *The Municipalities of the Roman Empire*) is significant: "My father led you down from the mountains to the plains; when you lived in scattered places he made you dwellers in cities, and he equipped you with institutions adapted to your changed mode of life." The last sentence sums up the task of a developing civilization, and it has a special importance in the history of the people that first made town planning an art.

The Roman Empire succeeded where Greece and the Hellenized East failed, for it established long spells of peace over a great part of the world. The Romans gained their Empire by their military prowess and their political genius, but for the purposes of this comparison military success is the least important thing about that Empire. It was not on that ground that St. Augustine in *De Civitate Dei* bade the citizens of the City of God look to Rome for lessons and inspiration. The secret of its power was its ability to satisfy and attach the races and classes that came under its rule. Of the evils and perils that this civilization overcame and survived, Roman history is full. We have only to recall some of the pictures given in Dr. Heitland's *Agricola*, Mommsen's saying that the sum of negro slavery was a drop in the bucket compared with the misery inflicted by the slave trade of Delos, the slave wars almost as horrible as the struggle between Carthage and her mercenary army after the first Punic War described by Flaubert in *Salammbô*, the brutalizing atmosphere of the amphitheatre, the Social War, the civil strife that so nearly put out the light of this civilization in the closing days of the Republic, to realize how remarkable an achievement it was for this social life to hold the Empire together during the centuries necessary to fix its foundations deep in the habits and mind of Europe. We know from such books as those of Dill, Reid, and Professor Rostovtzeff how stimulating and various an enjoyment of life was organized in the cities of the Empire; how great an importance was given to public beauty; how lavishly the rich, and even the middle classes, spent their money on theatres, baths, libraries, and temples; how widely, as Greenidge put it, the supply to the poor of what we call luxuries was deemed an obligation of wealth. The civilization of that Empire is known as Graeco-Roman just because it kept this Greek tradition and spread it under different forms all over the Western world.

How persistent was this tradition, even though the rulers of the State might differ as sharply as Augustus differed from Pericles, or the spirit of politics as sharply as those of fifth-century Athens and those of the Antonines, we can see when we remind ourselves that a man visiting Athens in the fifth century B.C., Rhodes in the second century B.C., and a Roman town in Africa or Spain in the second century A.D., would have noted that certain characteristics were common to all of them. First he would see that public beauty held a sovereign place in the ambitions and esteem of the time. The boast made by Smyrna when she claimed the title of " First City of Asia by beauty and importance, most brilliant and glory of Ionia," named the distinctions that every city, Greek, Hellenist, or Graeco-Roman, put first. The beauty of which cities were proud was not beauty hidden away in private houses, but beauty that the whole world could see and admire. An observation by a Greek sophist, Archytas of Tarentum, which Cicero quotes in his treatise

on Friendship, throws some light on their feeling about
it: "If a man should climb alone into heaven and look
upon the structure of the world and the beauty of the
stars, he would find no pleasure in that spectacle though
it would fill him with delight if he had someone to whom
he could speak of it." A hungry man coming on food
in a desert island would not say that he could not enjoy
that food because he was alone; Robinson Crusoe was
glad enough to eat before he had the company of Friday.
The sophist held then that the enjoyment of beauty is
not, like the enjoyment of food, an individual satisfaction; that it is connected in some way with man's social
nature. He held, that is, with some modern philosophers
that beauty is a reality which is perceived specially in the
contact between minds. It was perhaps this conviction
or this intuition that led the Greeks to realize the power
that beauty has over men's sympathies and imagination,
and in consequence to look upon beauty as essentially for
common enjoyment. Demosthenes reminded the Athens
of his days that Themistocles or Aristides lived in plain
houses indistinguishable from those of their neighbours,
and that the great buildings were to be found on the
Acropolis. Alcibiades outraged public sentiment by
painting his house. The Greeks then regarded beauty
as a spiritual power that could influence politics, helping
to make men generous and public-spirited, able to forget
in a common loyalty the passions that tended to drive
them and keep them apart. "Even a man whose soul
was utterly burdened," said Dion Chrysostom of Pheidias'
statue of Zeus at Olympia, "who had drained in his life
the cup of sorrow and misfortune and had not closed his
eyes in sleep, will forget, when he stands opposite this
statue, all the terrors and hardships of human life."

The second thing that such a visitor would have

noticed was the great proportion of expenditure in wealth and labour that was devoted to things that were for common enjoyment. This was illustrated not only by the beauty and grace of the public buildings, but also by the amenities that were brought within the reach of poor people. Every town had its theatres, its baths, its public games and festivals, its great gardens and colonnades. Many towns engaged public doctors, and sophists, philosophers, and grammarians were generally relieved of all public burdens. All this elaborate provision for the amusement of the mass of the population was made possible partly by the possession of common land and other common property, and partly by the fashion of private liberality for public objects. One of the first uses to which a rich man thought of putting his wealth was to adorn his city or to make an endowment that would associate his name and memory with its renown and the happiness and gratitude of its citizens; he would build a theatre or racecourse, or he would set aside a sum of money for education or for providing baths for the poor or for the slaves. He believed with Bacon that " riches are for spending and spending for honour and good actions."

The habits and tastes of the East spread to the West, and musical and literary exhibitions became common there, while gladiatorial shows and wild beast hunts penetrated to the East, not without protest from Plutarch and Lucian. Galen, the well-known medical writer, was physician to a troop of gladiators at Pergamum. There were still differences between East and West, for Greece never took whole-heartedly to the gladiatorial games, and the West never quite lost its contempt for the palaestra and the gymnasium. But in East and West alike the diversions offered to the mass of the population assumed an importance in expenditure and public life to which the modern world affords no parallel.

This truth is illustrated in the sermon on Poverty which Lucian put in the form of a dialogue between the cobbler and the cock inhabited by the soul of Pythagoras. Certain reflections are common to all the arguments by which philosophers and teachers have sought at different ages to persuade the poor thàt they are happier than the rich.   All touch on the pleasures or comforts of the body. Horace says that a rich man cannot hold more in his stomach than a poor man; Lucian contrasts the afflictions of the rich, gout, pneumonia, and other diseases due to intemperance, with the good health of the poor, who live on sprats and a bunch of onions; Paley reminds the poor man that if anything unusual comes his way he finds a feast, whereas the epicure dines too well every day to enjoy any novelty.   At all ages again philosophers have dwelt on the cares and responsibilities of the rich and powerful.   "You sleep well on a rug," said Martial to the slave, "your master lies awake on a bed of down." Lucian told the poor in a lively passage that the rich have to risk their lives in the field as commanders of horse or foot, "whereas you with but a wicker shield have little to carry and nothing to impede your flight and are ready to celebrate the victory when the general offers sacrifice after winning the battle."   Paley argues that the poor escaped the anxieties of the rich about their children. "All the provision which a poor man's child needs is contained in two words, industry and innocence."   These arguments are used to console the poor in all ages.   But we notice one important difference: whereas in the nineteenth century the argument runs that there is no capital without the rich, no production without capital, and no wages without production, Lucian put it that the rich had to toil that the poor might have baths, shows, and everything else, to their hearts' content. That is, whereas the modern economist put it that the poor man is indebted to the rich for his livelihood, the ancient moralist said that he was indebted to the rich for his luxuries.

The third feature of public life that such an observer would notice was the great part played in social life by voluntary associations. This was specially noticeable in the Roman Empire, where all classes were encouraged to form clubs and colleges, for the maintenance of their corporate dignity, the celebration of a patron or festival, or the organization of common pleasure or thrift, or to secure for the poorest and humblest person such a funeral as would not leave him an outcast in death. If the highest class had its group in the Curiales and the men who rose to wealth from the freedman class had their group in the Augustales, the lower classes of freedmen, artisans, and slaves, marched under their own flags in great processions to their special places at the games, and kept festivals and ceremonies at which, if only for a passing hour, the common life of the city seemed more important than all the inequalities of fortune. We know from the works of Dill and R. H. Barrow that in such a group a slave would sometimes preside over freedmen.

The Roman Empire depended on its power to satisfy the social imagination of its subjects, and it lasted as long as that power lasted. Montesquieu said that the Romans received slaves from all parts of the world and returned them as Romans. This, of course, is a picturesque exaggeration, but the phrase describes the Roman genius at its best, the kind of spirit that distinguishes and explains its success. It is not so much ironical as significant that the man who had to repeat Terence's famous declaration,

"Homo sum; humani nihil a me alienum puto," was a slave, acting in a play composed by a man who had first set foot in Rome as a slave. Compared with the Greeks the Romans were a brutal people, but they devised the political system by which the Greek tradition of humane, beautiful, and comforting life was kept alive and spread over Europe. Nothing in M. Rostovtzeff's pages is more interesting than his description of the efforts of the later Emperors to combat the dangers that threatened and finally extinguished the Empire, by creating new centres of city culture whence this gentle light might be cast over the passions of fierce neighbours and races that were still untamed. The history of the Empire, from a certain point of view, is the history of an euthanasia, the decay of a civilizing power, of which this municipal life had been the most conspicuous expression. If we may vary a phrase of Bacon's, we may say that the Romans had devised a plan under which men could be ruled by a despotism without putting off the generosity of their minds. Pelham said that this eager stirring city life was a substitute for politics. But there came a time when freedom and civilization were no longer united in fact or in illusion. A change passed over the life of the Empire. Diocletian's reorganization marked a stage in a decline. The cities lost their self-government; compulsory services supplied the needs of the State; the bureaucracy became all-powerful, and the Empire sought to satisfy the social imagination of the ruled by the pomp of its ceremonies and the sheer magnificence of its ruler.

No attempt has been made in these few pages to estimate the happiness and misery of the poor under Greek or Roman government; to calculate how far social amenities compensated for the privations and the cruelties to which they were exposed; to consider all the evils that a society suffers and inflicts if its basis is slavery; to trace the causes, so brilliantly discussed in the third volume of Toynbee's Study of History (*The Problem of the Growth of Civilizations*), of the fate that overtook " a thousand city-states, living side by side, in peace and concord." That is a task for scholars. The aim of this survey is different and more modest. It is to see what light we can draw from well-known facts about ancient history for our inquiry into the causes of social discontent in the nineteenth century. In the history of Graeco-Roman civilization we are watching the government, not of docile or acquiescent races, or of primitive and unsophisticated tribes, but of societies conspicuously intelligent, critical, and high-spirited. Or we may put it that we are watching experiments in group life which have a special value for all time, because we possess rich and illuminating records of the active and interesting peoples that were engaged in making them, and a literature in which those experiments are discussed, explained, and criticized, by acute and penetrating minds. In such a world the problem of making a stable society is not a problem set to force, but a problem set to wisdom; it is not an essay in terrorism, but an essay in statesmanship. The same problem was set to nineteenth-century England, for the English people were no more docile and acquiescent than the communities for whose satisfaction this elaborate city life was devised. And the Industrial Revolution which had spread far and wide the improvements that the economists describe, had put to that statesmanship problems not less subtle and difficult than the problems put to Augustus or the Antonines in the government of a Roman province.

CHAPTER III

THE NEW PROBLEM

There have been long ages in the history of the world when social life has been languid and impoverished, and yet there has been no revolt of which literature gives any record. Custom will reconcile men and women to conditions that they would find intolerable if they came fresh to them. For custom has a magic that takes the sting out of injustice, making it seem rather the decree of heaven than the sin of man. Thus the spell that custom casts on the imagination is the greatest conservative force in the world, a force so strong that it will keep life in institutions which have long ceased to serve, or even to remember, the purpose that brought them into use. As life follows its circle of unbroken routine no fierce questions are asked about facts and conditions that seem part of everyday experience, the face of a familiar world. When, therefore, society is passing through changes that destroy the life of custom, the statesman who seeks, in Bacon's words, to command man's will and not merely his deeds and services, has a specially difficult task, for those changes bring into men's minds the dreaded questions that have been sleeping beneath the surface of habit.

England at this time was passing through such changes. Some critics argue that the Industrial Revolution described by Toynbee has been pushed into a false importance. It is true that that revolution was a phase in a series of changes reaching far back into history. Some may put the beginning of the revolution on the day when Columbus set sail in his cockle shell to cross the Atlantic; others when Godfrey de Bouillon led crusaders and merchants to the Holy Land, bringing the West with its needs and energy once more into touch with the resources of the East; others will go back to the time when Cretan and Phoenician first learned how rich a basin holds the Mediterranean Sea. The student may take his choice. But whatever the date and whatever the cradle we name for this great event, it remains true that the England of this time was an England in movement, that speculation was in the air, that the indolent influence of habit was shaken, and that the statesman could no longer hope that half his work would be done for him by custom.

Another aspect of this age must be kept in mind. It was an age of energy and power, in which man eclipsed, in his new authority over nature, the spectacular triumphs of the architects and engineers of Rome. We can dig up to-day the bones of strong cities, which had once a vigorous and brilliant life in the waste of the African desert, desert when the Romans went there, desert to-day. Those buried columns speak of a miracle, but of a miracle less astonishing than the creation of the railway power that conquered distance, the obstacle that had so long arrested the development of Europe; less astonishing than the creation of the Lancashire cotton industry, its raw material brought across the Atlantic Ocean, its finished products carried round the Cape to India and the China Seas. There was no question here of a society drawing its ebbing breath under some stroke of disease or destiny. Man's power stared the new world in the face. In such an age the inequalities of life are apt to look less like

B

calamities from the hand of heaven and more like injustices from the hand of man.

Upon the society in whose manner of life and sense of power this change was taking place, there had fallen the shock of the French Revolution. We can measure the effect of that shock if we compare the world of ideas within which Wordsworth or Coleridge or Southey or Mill were moving when they reflected on the future of society, with that in which Gibbon was moving when he asked himself in a famous passage whether the civilized world might ever suffer again a calamity like the fall of the Western Empire. The dangers and the dreams that haunt the nineteenth-century thinkers never appear on his horizon. He looks out from a world composed and untroubled about its basis; they belonged to a world where the moral foundations of society, and the justice and the power of the bonds that unite its members, are the subject of vehement and incessant debate between hope and fear. No disappointment, however cold, could make the world after 1789 exactly what it was before, for intimations strange and alien to the eighteenth-century mind linger in the senses, although a blight had fallen on the first promise of " the greatest and best thing that had ever happened in the history of man." Between Gibbon and Wordsworth fear and hope had both passed through a revolution.

This was an atmosphere to excite thinkers and dreamers, and we know how quickly the active minds, philosophers and poets, turned to new problems in this crisis of our history. The atmosphere that produced Bentham and Godwin, Southey and Coleridge, Ricardo and Malthus, Shelley and Wordsworth, Mill and Carlyle, was certain to produce some intellectual movement in the working-class world. We see the result in the appear-

ance of thinkers and writers representing revolt in different aspects, Paine, Spence, Carlile, Hone, Hetherington,
Cobbett who idealized the past the peasant was losing,
and Lovett who idealized the future that he saw in the
workman's grasp. It has been said that when the licence
enjoyed by Gibbon was claimed by Carlile a new world
had taken to infidelity; so when Cobbett's " Twopenny
trash " succeeded to the Letters of Junius a new world
had taken to politics. The characteristic of this age was
the cheap pamphlet or paper written for the working
man. At first this literature found its audience chiefly
among London shoemakers, small tradesmen, and artisans, but in time it spread to the miners and the mill
workers; Lancashire was for Church and King in 1793,
but for radical reform in 1819. It was said in the exaggeration of panic of *The Black Dwarf*, published by
Wooler the Yorkshire printer who migrated to London,
that in one northern district in 1819 it was to be found
in the crown of the hat of almost every pitman you met.
Ten years later the mills used to turn out when the
London coach brought Cobbett's *Register* to the Lancashire towns. The first paper was published in London,
but the provincial towns soon followed. Manchester had
a *Wardle's Manchester Observer*; Birmingham, *Edwards'
Weekly Register*; Coventry its *Recorder*; Dudley its
Patient. In addition to the better-known papers, like
Carlile's *Gauntlet*, Detroisier's *Cosmopolitan*, the Spen-
cean paper *Man*, the Owenite paper *The Crisis*, the
Working Man's Friend, there were several unstamped
papers in the country, especially in Manchester, Leeds,
Bradford, and such towns, taking their tone from the
Poor Man's Guardian, owned by Hetherington and edited
by Bronterre O'Brien. The *Pioneer* was the organ of the
Builders' movement in the early thirties; Doherty ran

The Voice of the People and the *Poor Man's Advocate*; and in 1837 Feargus O'Connor started the most successful of all the democratic papers, the *Northern Star*. Of the wild hopes about this new force that inspired democrats at the time, we have an illustration in the concluding verse of Ebenezer Elliott's poem, *The Press*:

> " ' The Press ' all lands shall sing,
> The Press, the Press we bring,
>   All lands to bless!
> O pallid want!   O labour stark,
> Behold we bring the second ark,
>   The Press, the Press, the Press."

To understand what forces were ready to gather behind these rebel or these building minds, we must remember that the new towns were drawing into factory and slum men and women who had themselves passed through a revolution. Mr. Redford says that the census returns for 1851 show that in almost all the great towns the migrants from elsewhere outnumbered the people born in the town. Now the industrial towns were growing at a great pace. We can get an idea of the pace if we take the census figures for three years, 1801, 1831, and 1851, for some of the towns of Lancashire and the West Riding. The figures for Manchester and Salford are roughly 90,000, 237,000, 400,000; for Leeds, 53,000, 123,000, 172,000; for Sheffield, 46,000, 92,000, 135,000; for Bradford, 13,000, 44,000, 104,000; for Oldham, 22,000, 51,000, 72,000; for Bolton, 18,000, 42,000, 61,000; for Blackburn, 12,000, 27,000, 65,000; for Halifax, 12,000, 22,000, 34,000. In all these towns and in many others a great proportion of the inhabitants had changed their home, their occupation, and their surroundings. Now the Industrial Revolution seen in the perspective of the life of the world may seem a gradual process, so gradual that economists find fault with the phrase as inexact. But as an experience in the individual and family lives of the men and women drawn into Manchester or Bradford, the Industrial Revolution was sudden and its consequences sweeping. The revolution that had given them a new home and a new manner of life would not have lost its sharp taste if the economist had explained to them that large-scale production was known in the ancient world, and that specialized industry had once enriched Babylon and Damascus just as it was then enriching Manchester and Bradford. The towns had now large populations of men and women who had passed from the life of the village to the life of the slum; from the occupations of the peasant to those of the urban worker.

The new population was mainly composed of people born and bred in the country. Wordsworth said that the invention of the steam engine had saved the countryside, for mills could now be built in the ugly towns instead of spoiling the streams and valleys. For the country people turned into slum dwellers the change was less fortunate. They had not lost their instincts and longings or their sense for beauty and peace. Some observers think that we are paying the penalty to-day for making our towns unsightly in the destruction of our landscape by a town people in whom the sense for beauty has been killed. It was feared in the thirties that if London people found themselves in a park or garden the " propensity to mischief" would assert itself with disastrous results. In the North, on the other hand, where the workman's memories of his country life were still alive, observers noticed with astonishment that this propensity was kept in check. When Lord Stamford threw open his park on a Sunday the workpeople of Manchester flocked there, making the journey in many cases on foot, and the park suffered no damage at the hands of 20,000 visitors. Sir Joseph Paxton told the Committee on Public-Houses in 1854 that the Duke of Devonshire allowed excursionists from Birmingham, Nottingham, Leicester, and Leeds to visit Chatsworth, and that their behaviour was most orderly. " As many as 1,000 or 1,200 people go round at a time and in no instance have we found any difficulty arise. . . ." " We had only one man or perhaps two over the whole premises to look after them; and the people behaved exceedingly well." The love of nature dies hard. Faucher, a French visitor, said that one of the evils of which the poor were most conscious in Leeds was the smoke that destroyed their little window gardens.

Nor was the loss of beauty the only discomfort these immigrants suffered. Wordsworth has described the lone shepherd on a promontory,

> " Who lacking occupation looks far forth
> Into the boundless sea and rather makes
> Than finds what he beholds."

Nature gives some play to the fancy of the peasant as his eye wanders slowly over field and woodland, and though we picture him with a simple mind, town life, to make him happy, has to find some substitute for the satisfaction that the lone shepherd found in his promontory looking far forth into the boundless sea. For the first half of the nineteenth century the industrial town was absorbing the English peasant used to an open-air life, learning from the landscape, in touch with nature, moving and thinking with its gentle rhythm, making rather than finding what he beheld.

The towns were thus receiving a large population strange to town life in habits and experience. But there was an even more disturbing element in the problem now set to governments and magistrates, to architects and engineers, to doctors, schoolmasters, and ministers of religion. If you went to Manchester or Leeds, or to the smaller towns like Oldham or Stalybridge, you would find that the immigrants were in the main either countrymen from the same or a neighbouring county, or Irishmen and Irishwomen. It was easier to reach Lancashire and Yorkshire from Ireland than from Norfolk or Dorset. A Wiltshire peasant would have to make his way North by coach or canal boat or wagon, or on foot. The labourers who were sent to Lancashire by the Poor Law authorities were taken to London, put on a boat of Pickford's at the Paddington basin of the Grand Junction Canal, and carried to Manchester in four or five days at a cost of fourteen shillings. But an Irishman could cross to Liverpool for half a crown in fourteen hours; in 1827 fierce competition brought down the price to fourpence or fivepence.

Now Ireland so dangerously near to Lancashire was an uncomfortable neighbour. For the Irish peasant was the victim of unexampled misgovernment and neglect. "In no other country," said *The Times*, "have the wealth of the proprietor, the power of the magistrate and the accomplishments of the educated, been employed less for the benefit of the many, more for the gain and the pleasure of the few." Consequently the Irish immigration had a special character. Sir George Cornewall Lewis pointed out that the Greeks and Phoenicians settling in the Mediterranean, the Spaniards and the English settling in the New World, went from a more to a less civilized community. The Fleming woollen weavers, the Huguenot silk weavers, the German tailors, brought to England, the English mechanics took to France, a special skill.

" But the Irish emigration into Britain is an example of a less civilized population spreading themselves as a kind of substratum beneath a more civilized community."

This Irish substratum composed in 1841 a tenth of the population of Manchester and a seventh of the population of Liverpool. At that time the Irish population in Lancashire was over 133,000. But after the failure of the potato in the forties, the event that precipitated the repeal of the Corn Laws and the break-up of the Conservative party, the flood became a deluge. It has been calculated that 500,000 Irish people entered Great Britain between 1841 and 1851. By the later date the Irish population in Lancashire had nearly reached 200,000, swollen by the refugees flying from the famine that destroyed nearly a million lives in Ireland. " During the last two or three months," wrote the registrar of a Manchester district, " large numbers of the poor from Ireland have crowded themselves in this district, droves of them rambling about the streets seeking lodgings and no doubt being exposed to the severe and inclement weather. Many of the poor creatures have died from cold producing fevers and diseases." At Liverpool there were " thousands of hungry and naked Irish perishing in our streets," and in South Wales they were described as " bringing pestilence on their backs, famine in their stomachs."

Thus the dirtiness and disorder of the squalid English town were now increased by the presence of a large body of Irish people who lived normally under conditions repugnant to their English neighbours.

This had two serious consequences. In the first place, the greatest blot on the towns where the Irish settled was the cellar-dwelling. The immigrants crowded into these cellars, and as there was no check on the speculative builder, cellars were built in great numbers with the confident expectation of finding tenants for them. This was not the only evil that was prolonged and extended by the Irish immigration. The Irish immigrants in Lancashire, competing with a more skilled population, were confined as a rule to the coarser and less eligible employments. Among the occupations from which English workmen were turned away because its wages and prospects were steadily declining was that of handloom weaving. The Irish resorted to this failing industry and drew out its slow and painful death.

In these ways the Irish immigration was a burden on towns where filth and poverty were already unmanageable problems. But it brought also the friction that is inevitable when immigrant labourers can underbid the natives. As Irishmen were often bricklayers' labourers, and as they had been employed a good deal on road-making and canal-cutting, they were specially suitable for such work as railway construction. But by the late thirties, when railway projects were in great favour, trade depression had brought unemployment and there were riots in several places when attempts were made to introduce Irish labour. More than once such riots became battles, and it was often found impossible to put English and Irish to work together. That the Irish were used to keep down wages and to break strikes was admitted by textile employers, and Irish labour was brought over from Ireland for this purpose by a silk manufacturer at Newton Heath and by cotton spinners at Preston. The employers, however, regarded Irish workmen with mixed feelings, and they spoke of them sometimes much as a Roman master used to speak of the slaves from turbulent Sardinia. " The Irish," said one employer, " are more disposed to turn out, to make unreasonable demands, to

take offence at slight cause and to enforce their demands
by strikes or bad language." A Catholic priest said that
he had noticed that the Irish were more prone than the
English to take part in trade unions, and he attributed
this to habits acquired under the bad laws of Ireland.
Whether this or the Celtic temperament was the cause,
it is undoubtedly true that Ireland gave several leaders to
the English workmen, the most notable of them being, of
course, the celebrated John Doherty, the founder of the
strongest union of the time, whose services to reform must
be set against the squalor that his countrymen brought
with them. The discord due to economic friction was
inflamed by religious differences. Nobody can study the
papers of this time without seeing how widespread and
violent were the religious quarrels of the industrial towns.

The towns, then, to whom it fell to act as the civilizing
influence in this new society were largely inhabited by
men and women who were country people by experience,
taste, and habit, and in respect of great numbers, alien
in history, religion, and race. But it was not only in this
way that this population felt the strain of change. There
was at the same time a revolution in the life and rhythm
of industry. English industry before this time was un-
methodical. Bouts of work and bouts of play used often
to alternate, violent play following violent work. Bam-
ford has described the Christmas festivals of his young
days when beer was brewed and spice-cake baked, and
the weavers, young and old, kept at work night and day
to finish their tasks so that the days after Christmas might
be free for feasting and revelry. Even in ordinary times
whole days rather than hours in a day were given to
recreation. The Sheffield journeymen were said to work
only three days in the week. This is probably an exaggeration, but the custom of taking days off even when

work was plentiful survived in non-factory industry. Thus the framework knitters at Hinckley sat at their work for thirteen to sixteen hours a day, never getting into the open air till twelve on Saturday, when the work was sent to the warehouse and they stopped completely till Tuesday. Monday was market day, and the workers were fagged out. In the Potteries, too, the custom survived, and in the country districts round Coventry the ribbon weavers, however poor they were, were said in 1840 to "absent themselves from work nearly the whole of Saturday, Sunday, the whole of Monday and a little of Tuesday," working excessively hard for the rest of the week, including often the whole of Friday night. These outbursts of work and play were uneconomical, and, where machinery was introduced, a new system of work was obviously necessary. Improved methods of production involved the training of the working population in orderly and regular habits. Fines regulated every detail of conduct. To people accustomed to the irregular and undisciplined atmosphere of the old industry, the system of fines in the mills seemed gross tyranny.

Here, then, were all the elements of a difficult social problem. The towns were the homes of workmen, once artisans with scope for their instinct to express and create, who had passed into the impersonal routine of the mill; of men and women with peasant outlook and tradition, accustomed to the peace and beauty of nature, shut up in slum and alley; of immigrants from a land of deadly poverty, bringing their own habits and religion into a society struggling with dirt and torn by sectarian strife. All of these types were being drawn into new associations, creating and receiving the influence of new group atmospheres. We know to-day how subtle and powerful is the influence of what Mazzini called "collective intuitions."

The new town had thus to satisfy the spiritual needs of men and women wrestling with the most difficult of all spiritual adjustments, forming a new social mind, disturbed by changes that had destroyed the basis of custom in their lives. The evidence of man's power in the world was impressive and ubiquitous. The contrasts that religion had to justify, the inequalities that culture had to reconcile, were glaring and provocative. How was this society placed for that task? On what did it rely to draw these various elements together in mutual sympathy and confidence?

CHAPTER IV

THE REMEDY OF THE NEW WORLD

INDIVIDUAL OPPORTUNITY

THIS society was not blind to the danger of discontent, nor was it unaware of the reasons for expecting that discontent to increase. De Quincey has an interesting passage in his description of his early life at Greenheys in Manchester about what he called personal Jacobinism. He and his brother, when on their way to school, used to meet a number of mill boys who called them " bucks " and pelted them with stones because they wore Hessian boots. De Quincey adds that however angry they were made by his aristocratic dress, the youths from the mill had no sympathy with political Jacobinism and would shout readily enough for Church and King. Their personal Jacobinism, he explained, was " of that sort which is native to the heart of man, who is by natural impulse (and not without a root of nobility, though also of base envy) impatient of inequality, and submits to it only through a sense of its necessity, or under a long experience of its benefits." De Quincey was speaking of the opening years of the century. Long before 1830 it had become evident that this personal Jacobinism was developing into political Jacobinism, and the problem of disarming or repressing this political Jacobinism had become the main care of the Governments of the time.

It did not follow because those Governments neglected the methods used for this purpose by ancient societies that they had no methods of their own.

To understand what those methods were it is convenient to return to Bacon's distinction between rulers who seek to command the wills of men and those who seek only to command their deeds and services. The distinction is roughly between governments that seek to rule with the help of the imagination of the ruled, and those that seek to rule without it. That distinction divides both governments and politicians. In England in the early nineteenth century both schools were represented by men of vigour, courage, and tenacity. Both schools had been greatly strengthened by the French Revolution, which had confirmed in their convictions both the school that trusted entirely to force and the school that believed in governing men by persuasion.

The school of force refused to admit that society could be made happier or more stable by attempting to create a spiritual sympathy between government and governed, between class and class. A spokesman of this school, say Castlereagh or Sidmouth, would have said, if asked to explain his philosophy, something like this: " Life for the mass of men and women must inevitably be hard, bleak, and painful. Poverty is bearable by those who are used to it. Great economic and social changes are upsetting the life of custom, which is the life of acquiescence. For that very reason let us cling more closely to custom, where it can still be preserved, custom in government, custom in religion, custom in law. After all, the mass of men have obedience in their bones. The moment you begin to reform your capital institutions you destroy the attachment of custom, and you cannot make sure that you are going to create in its place ties of affection or confidence. Keep, therefore, what you have: an unreformed Parliament, unreformed law, unreformed Church, a landed aristocracy maintained by the Corn Laws. Use these institutions to make disobedience terrible to those who are tempted into it. But keep temptation out of their way. Do not let any disturbing or stimulating influence reach this subject population. Put down the cheap press; shut up agitators; leave the poor ignorant, or if you must teach them give them only such an education as will put the fear of God and of the magistrates into their hearts. The more the inequalities of life increase the more essential is it to see that government rests on an adequate force of power, tradition and the prestige that belongs to superior culture. Look to this, and do not flatter your fancy with dreams of *populi volentes.*" This school, strongly represented among politicians, churchmen, and magistrates, in the first twenty years of the century, had a powerful influence on the life of the times. It sought to crush the cheap press and popular propaganda by imposing heavy stamp duties on all periodicals, it put men in prison freely for distributing pamphlets and books, and Sidmouth would have liked to suppress all reading-rooms. At this time, as Dr. Hook said later, every sermon preached on behalf of a charity school had to prove that no harm would be done in educating the poor.

This school survived, of course, after 1830, but no longer as a political party; it was a die-hard faction. You would have found among landlords, manufacturers, magistrates, parsons, and other persons of influence, men who thought like Sidmouth and Castlereagh. But Peel, who led the Conservative party until he destroyed it, had nothing in common with this sentiment; he differed from a Tory like Sidmouth more than he differed from a

Radical like Hume. The Conservative party in his hands was a party of reform, not of repression. Men disagreed in the value they put on existing institutions; on attachment to Church or squire; on the uses of custom or the dangers of change. But none of the greater leaders of thought or of politics would have held that their society could be ruled without the help of its imagination. Wordsworth or Coleridge, Maurice or Arnold, Carlyle or Mill, Peel or Russell, Bentham or Southey, all of them in their plans for improving or regulating the world rejected the garrison system of Sidmouth and Castlereagh, and aimed at commanding the wills and not merely the deeds of the ruled. The motives of loyalty or ambition, of sympathy or reverence, these, and not the spirit of fear, were the forces to which the guiding minds looked for the salvation of their society.

Among the ideas of the time one predominated in the practical life of the time. It was the belief that the Industrial Revolution had discovered the best remedy for discontent. For it offered to the poor man something to take his imagination; something to stimulate the element of nobility in the personal Jacobinism described by De Quincey, and to discourage the base envy that embittered it. It offered to him the prospect of ceasing to be a poor man. Men dominated by this excitement about the Industrial Revolution naturally held that society should arrange its institutions in such a way as to take full advantage of the new opportunities. " Remove all obstacles," they would have said, " to the spirit of initiative and enterprise. Encourage thrift; make it easy for capital and labour to move from industry to industry, from place to place; get rid of the Corn Laws which check the free exchange of goods; abolish abuses in State and Church; remove the dead-weight of custom wherever it checks

1an's energy and spirit; spread education. Then you
vill see what the Industrial Revolution can do to give
ou a rich and a happy instead of a poor and discontented
eople. Give this clear field to the Industrial Revolution,
nd the steam engines and the railway will take care of
ociety." For the Industrial Revolution had put a new
adder within the reach of diligence and worth. Never
.ad men passed with steps so sure and swift from poverty
o wealth, from obscurity to renown. To recite the
ames on this new roll of fame, from Brindley to
tephenson, from Davy to Arkwright, from Telford to
'eel, is like reciting the names of Napoleon's field-
marshals, from Hoche to Murat, from Ney to Bernadotte.
een in this light, the cotton industry offered to the
nglish workman the prospect that the revolutionary
rmies had offered to the French peasant. When did
hrift, enterprise, and intelligence reap such reward?

It is true that men had found their way in other ages
rom insignificance to power; that starting within the
Roman slave system a man might become a great bureau-
rat, a great doctor, a great man of letters; that inscrip-
ions tell us of a senator and censor who began life as a
clodhopper, of towns adorned and paved by rich men
vho had once crept along their streets behind a master
with power of life and death; that in the Middle Ages
he Church offered an escape from the drudgery of the
soil to such men as the Minister Suger, or Pope Silvester II;
hat in the sixteenth and seventeenth centuries banking
and commerce could turn plain homespun material into
something that would pass for the finished product of a
proud and ancient line. But where in other ages there
had been room for one man on this golden staircase, there
was now room for a hundred. A merchant or a spinner
like Gould or Cobden moved in a world where it was

more likely than not that the first rich man he met had been born poor, and was, in Tiberius' phrase, his own ancestor.

It was not only the railway king or the cotton lord who symbolized this triumphant principle for the optimists of the age. Cobden was enthusiastic about the ease with which a thrifty man could make himself independent without luck or genius. " I would then," he said in a famous letter, " advise the working classes to make themselves free of the labour market of the world, and this they can do by accumulating twenty pounds each, which will give them the command of the only market in which labour is at a higher rate than in England—I mean that of the United States. If every working man would save this sum, he might be as independent of his employer as the latter, with his great capital, is of his workmen." So simple a sacrifice was all that was needed to make the man who to-day looked the slave of his circumstances, a person of standing, choosing his employment and his employer.

Thus individual success took in this society the place that common enjoyment had taken in the ancient world. The business man pointing to the triumphant career of the Lancashire cotton spinner, with " nitor in adversum " for his family motto, would have argued that there was here a more inspiring spectacle, a truer sign of human progress, than a theatre at Olympia, crowded with Greeks of every class listening to a chorus of the " Agamemnon." This ideal had the glamour and freshness that belonged to a new religion, for it was associated with the great emancipating truths that the world had learnt from the French and American Revolutions. The freedom to make the most of yourself in competition with your fellow men seemed to the Englishman of the age the

most important of all the personal rights that those
Revolutions had proclaimed and vindicated. This right
marked a great step forward in the history of mankind.
As individualism dethroned feudalism, the prestige of
work dethroned the prestige of idleness. Now the
prestige of idleness had been one of the curses of the
world. From time to time it had been shaken. The
monks, building their monasteries with their own hands,
had put to shame the false pride that made a Roman
think it less disgraceful to depend upon a State or upon
a patron than to earn his living by the labour he called
sordid. But the prestige of idleness had persisted
through the world's history, and eighteenth-century
England maintained gentlemen of good families, living
on pensions and sinecures, who thought themselves
morally superior to anyone who worked for his living.
Herodotus explained why industrial occupations were
despised in the ancient world in comparison with occupations or modes of life that fitted men and States for war.
Manchester reflected the new light in which this false
perspective had been destroyed: war and industry had
changed places. What was the history of progress but
the history of man's advance from a world in which
wealth and power had been seized by those who had
conquered and plundered their fellows, to a world in
which they had been earned by those who supplied the
wants of mankind? It had been a great day in that
history when the merchants of Venice and the bankers of
Florence were strong enough to make themselves the
rivals of feudal lords and royal princes. With the new
prestige of production a still more brilliant day had
dawned. When men admired the Peels and the Ark-
wrights, they would soon estimate at their true value the
Bourbons and Napoleons, the great drones or the great

pirates, who had once cast such a fatal spell on the human mind.

The Manchester merchant would have argued also that the new industrial system had given the English people a flexible society. Movement from class to class is a sign of a healthy social life. Men were rising in the world in Cobden's Manchester by hard work, prudent abstinence, shrewd sense, and inspired daring. How had men risen in other ages? What were the arts by which slave and ex-slave had made their way to independence and power in the Roman State? Listen to Juvenal or to Tacitus on the climbing freedman. When a weak Emperor was on the throne, or a strong Emperor lost his power of will, the Roman Empire slipped into the hands of favourites and had all the look of a degenerate Oriental state. Seneca has described Claudius giving an order in heaven: "You might have imagined they were all his own freed-men: so little notice did they take of him." When the worst had been said about the forces and qualities that brought a man to the front in the early scramble of the Industrial Revolution, this method of promotion was at least to be preferred to the arts by which many a Roman Prefect had become a power in the government of the Roman Empire. The system which had made Peel the master of the House of Commons need not fear compari-son with the system which made a Pallas the master of the Senate.

Let anybody, again, compare this industrial England with feudal England: Manchester with the villages of Dorset and Wilts. Here men rose by their merit and by their own efforts. A man who saved a few pounds could put his best foot foremost without touching his cap to any of the powerful men on whose pleasure Crabbe, or Porson, or Clare had had to wait. And the most active

888888888888888888

minds of the time had no liking for the historical institutions through whose doors poor men in other ages had passed to fame. Those institutions from the Church downwards were as remarkable at this time for their abuses as their virtues, and the spirit of the age welcomed as the solution of most of the problems of life an arrangement which seemed to make the individual his own master, and to reduce in proportion the prestige and the power of the institutions that offered at once discipline and shelter to those who would step across their threshold. The man who in other ages wished to follow in the footsteps of Wolsey had to put on the cassock of a church, but a Peel or an Arkwright could become a millionaire without the surrender of conscience or freedom to anybody's keeping. This was the novelty that fascinated men like Cobden. They contrasted this world in which men needed no patron, with the world where everything depended on the smile of squire or parson, much as Lucian contrasted the free life of Athens with the degrading atmosphere of Rome, where flatterers courted the rich, and spoke to them as slaves spoke to a master.

Not least, perhaps, of the advantages that the Manchester merchant would have claimed for his age would have been its success in turning aside from the frivolities of the ancient world. For he would have regarded the social life of the Roman Empire as a warning rather than an example. Where had that social life ended? Dion Chrysostom scolded the people of Alexandria for their wild excitement over horse-racing. "For cities are not only taken when men demolish their walls, kill the men, enslave the women, and burn their houses. When there is indifference to all that is noble, and a passion for one ignoble end: when men devote themselves and their time to it, dancing, mad, hitting each other, using unspeakable language, often blaspheming, gambling their possessions, and sometimes returning in beggary from the spectacle, that is the disgraceful and ignominious sack of a town." Amid the orgies of the theatre at Carthage in the fourth century A.D., when Genseric's Vandals were outside the walls, "confundebatur vox morientium voxque bacchantium." Gibbon has drawn a graphic picture of the violence of the factions of the circus at Byzantium and the fierce and bloody contests of green and blue that distracted the politics of the Eastern Empire. A sober merchant of Manchester would have laughed at the suggestion that his town, busy from rising to setting sun increasing the riches and comforts of the world, had anything to learn from a civilization that had degenerated into these scenes of outrage and discord; in which production had never been given its true import-ance, enjoyment had been allowed to run wild, and the men who served mankind the worst received the highest honours. Happy the new age in which success was so clearly the reward of merit, and private wealth and public benefit were so fortunately united. We have now to see what kind of town was created by these ideas; what was its education, its religion, its culture, and its social life.

CHAPTER V

THE LOSS OF COMMON ENJOYMENT

" At Glasgow, Liverpool and the like there is little else than the stench of trade." MILL to CARLYLE, March 1833, *Letters*, I, 38.

A VISITOR coming from the ancient world to Manchester and Leeds in 1830 would have been struck by their wealth, but he would have noticed that it was wealth owned by private persons and displayed, where it was displayed, in private magnificence. For though the new Englishman was richer than the Greek or the Roman, the new English city was poorer than the Greek or Roman city: poorer in its looks, its possessions, its ambitions, and the range and dignity of its desires and enjoyments. The new town had no share in the arts or culture of the time. De Quincey said at the beginning of the century that no great city could present so repulsive an appearance as the Manchester of his day. Lyon Playfair told the Health of Towns Commission in 1844 that in all Lancashire there was only one town, Preston, with a public park, and only one, Liverpool, with public baths. Popular theatres and galleries, public libraries and museums were almost unknown. So late as 1850 William Ewart, the leader of the movement for civilizing town life, told the House of Commons that large and populous towns like Sheffield and Leeds were without public libraries of any kind. There were few public spectacles, festivals, or amusements to draw classes together: the rich

and well-to-do had music, theatres, and games of their
own; the poor moved outside their orbit.

This society was described at the time by three observers,
each of them interesting because education or experience
had given him a background against which to set this
civilization. One was Dr. Arnold, a student of classical
history, steeped in its spirit and lessons; another was a
German, named Raumer, Professor of History at Berlin
University, who visited England in 1835; the third, a
Frenchman named Léon Faucher, who visited England
ten years later.

All three observers agreed that the poor man in
England had certain advantages over the poor man on the
Continent, and that he had a share in the benefits brought
by the agrarian and industrial revolutions. " The English
workmen and mechanics eat, drink, and are clothed better
than any others," wrote Raumer. Dr. Arnold pointed
out that " Earthenware has succeeded to wood or pewter;
their wives and children can dress better and cheaper,
and cheap publications are more numerous." But they
were all struck by the social incoherence of these towns,
their cold unhappiness, the class division of interests and
pleasures, the concentration on a limited and limiting
purpose. Faucher pointed out that the industrial towns
of France, such as Rouen and Lyons, were not specialized
populations; the law in Rouen, the Church in Lyons,
made their mark on the life and manners of the community. " But at Manchester industry has found no
previous occupant, and knows nothing but itself. Everything is alike, and everything is new. There is nothing
but masters and operatives." Raumer wrote, after visiting Leeds and Sheffield: " We therefore rarely trace any
comprehensive plan, any attention to general conveni-
ence, or to beauty and architectonic art. Capital is

employed solely in the creation of new capital. What is not calculated to promote this end is regarded as useless and superfluous. It is with a far different view that the west side of London has been enlarged." Arnold described this concentration in a letter to the *Sheffield Courant*. " Our great manufacturing towns have risen solely with a view to this relation of employers and employed. The very name shows this, that they are places where men have assembled together, not for the purposes of social life, but to make calicoes or hardware or broadcloth. A man sets up a factory and *wants hands*; I beseech you, sir, to observe the very expressions that are used, for they are all significant. What he wants of his fellow creatures is the loan of their hands; of their heads and hearts he thinks nothing."

The absence of amenities made a great impression on observers who could compare English life with the life of the Continent. Faucher remarked that the city authorities at Liverpool had prohibited cheap theatres, with the consequence that the poor had to amuse themselves in the tavern or at religious and political meetings, according to their taste. " If the people of Manchester want to go out on a Sunday," he asked, " where must they go? There are no public promenades, no avenues, no public gardens, and no public common . . . everything in the suburbs is closed against them; everything is private property; in the midst of the beautiful scenery of England the operatives are like the Israelites of old, with the promised land before them, but forbidden to enter into it."

The lack of common pleasure which made so strong an impression on these observers struck some far-sighted men in the House of Commons, and in 1833 a Select Committee was appointed to consider the deficiency of

"Public Walks and Places of Exercise." The facts were presented to Parliament by this Committee. "As respects those employed in the three great Manufactures of the Kingdom, Cotton, Woollen, and Hardware, creating annually an immense Property, no provision has been made to afford them the means of healthy exercise or cheerful amusement with their families on their Holidays or days of rest." Nor did the Committee find other large towns in any better case. Of all but a very few they wrote: "With a rapidly increasing Population, lodged for the most part in narrow courts, and confined streets, the means of occasional exercise and recreation in the fresh air are every day lessened, as inclosures take place and buildings spread themselves on every side." This neglect, suggested the Committee, might be due to preoccupation with the late war. A century later it is easy to see that this is too simple an explanation, and that there were strong forces at work which public opinion, even when unpreoccupied, was powerless to control.

In a community where there is plenty of waste land, and games are rude and uncomplicated, those who wish to play can easily find a playground. The people who live near what is called a common have no doubt that they can use it for recreation, whether stock is turned out on it or not by the Lord of the Manor and commoners. No questions of legal ownership trouble their minds. The difficulties begin when land rises in value, for legal rights then become important and the inhabitants become aware, from painful experience, of what has been called "the difference between popular conceptions and traditions and legal rights and conclusions."

According to the legal view which ignored ancient tradition and relied upon the imposition of the feudal system as the starting-point of common rights, all rights of common came from the grant or permission of the Lord of the Manor who owned the soil of the common or waste. It might have been argued that since the lord owned the soil in virtue of a grant which carried with it the performance of certain duties, the whole position should have been revised when those duties lapsed. But it was not revised, and in the eyes of the law the framework of feudalism still stood intact. Common rights, the right of use and the right of access, came into being, said the law, because at some time or other the lord had granted his tenants the right to graze cattle or sheep or to cut wood or turf on the waste of the lord's manor. It was then from the lord's grant or permission or sufferance that all common rights were derived.

Now, in a famous case in 1603 (Gatewards case) it was laid down that these rights could not be held by the inhabitants of a village or district merely as inhabitants. The term, said the judges, was too vague; common rights could only be held by owners of property. " According to the strict technical law," said Lord Eversley, " invented by the feudal lawyers—and superseding a much wider and more popular law, under which undoubtedly the commons were the common property of the village or community—the commons were the property of the Lords of Manors, and the tenants of their manors, and the public had no right to them, no matter how long or how much they had used them for recreation, no matter how necessary they might be for the health of the district." The legal position was clearly put by a member of the 1844 Committee: " Notwithstanding that all the world are in the habit of walking about on commons, and turning themselves on, in fact they have not acquired any legal right by that, but, practically, they would lose something if they were deprived of it."

An illustration will show that this legal interpretation of the rights of property put into the hands of the land-owners in many places an almost unlimited power of depriving a community of its customary places for walks and games. We will take the case of Basford. In this small framework knitting town, a few miles north of Nottingham, with 1,200 acres of forests, commons, and waste lands at its doors, the inhabitants before 1793 probably never thought about their playgrounds or wondered how they had been provided. They took them as a matter of course. After 1793 there were no play-grounds to think about, for an Inclosure Act swept the whole area into private hands. The inhabitants of Basford did not easily adapt themselves to the changed conditions. Fifty years later it was stated that the want of open land for recreation was "a fruitful source of bickering and recrimination between the young men of the parish and the owners and occupiers of lands, tres-passes on the part of the young men, for the purposes of cricket-playing and other games, being very common. There are now no common lands belonging to the parish. Formerly there were very extensive grounds of this class, but in 1793 these rights were resumed and the grounds enclosed, but without leaving a single acre for the use of the public."

At Basford the disaster was catastrophic; in other cases, Sheffield for example, the process was spread over several years. In that town by four separate Acts of Parliament, the first passed in 1779, the last in 1810, not less than 7,350 acres of common and waste lands were enclosed without a single rod, pole or perch being set apart for public recreation. Enclosure of one common was made easier by the fact that a second remained open; enclosure of the second made easier by the precedent of the first.

Enclosure Acts, it may be noted, were usually justified on the ground that the land was in its present state "incapable of improvement," whereas, if enclosed and handed over to private ownership, it would yield bounteous harvests. Round towns the big proprietors, and sometimes the small ones too, easily persuaded themselves that crops of villas (or slums, as the case may be) were as desirable to grow as crops of corn. Incidentally they were even more profitable to the grower.

How little the need for recreation had been recognized in the growing districts, is illustrated in the case of enclosures at Bolton, Oldham, and Gateshead. A great deal of waste was enclosed in East Lancashire before this time, in the sixteenth and seventeenth centuries, by agreement or moral compulsion. Didsbury Moor, Withington Moor, Kersal Moor, and Chorlton Moor, and other waste land near Manchester, had been enclosed by the eighteenth century. But there were Acts for enclosing waste at Bolton and Oldham at the time when these towns were growing very rapidly. The Bolton Act, dated 1792, contains rare, if not unique, provisions for applying the proceeds of enclosure to public purposes. Unfortunately recreation was not amongst those purposes. Although Great and Little Bolton were described in the Act as "large, populous, and trading Towns, and daily increasing," they were still large villages surrounded by open country. The Act directed that the 270 acres of Bolton Moor should be enclosed, and, after allotment of one acre for stone, and one-fifteenth for the Lords of the Manor, should be divided up into lots of not more than four acres and sold for 5,000 years for the best annual rent offered, subject to the immediate payment of £10 an acre. The money was to be spent by trustees, who were given large powers by the Act, on widening, paving, lighting, watching, cleansing, and otherwise improving the streets of Great Bolton, and on supplying water for the free use of the inhabitants. Any surplus was to go towards the Poor Rates. Seventy-one trustees were appointed to administer the Act, forty-one for Great Bolton, with a residential qualification of £1,000, and thirty for Little Bolton, with a qualification of £500. Two other Enclosure Acts of the usual type swallowed up other moor land in the Bolton district; Chew Moor (68 acres) was enclosed in 1807, Tonge Moor (acreage not stated) in 1812. In neither case was any allotment made for recreation. The result was described in 1833. " The population of Bolton being nearly 45,000, there are no public walks, or open spaces in the nature of walks, or public gardens reserved at all in its vicinity? "— " No." But, though no part of the moor was reserved for the purpose, games were still allowed on sufferance on ground that was technically enclosed.

The case of Oldham is specially interesting. An area of 300 Lancashire acres (that is, about 480 ordinary acres), consisting of Green Acres Moor, North Moor, Hollingwood, and other commons and wastes, was inclosed in 1802 without any allotment for recreation. Public interests, however, were not ignored, for 16 acres were allotted for a workhouse. It happened that Oldham was already well provided in this respect, and the land so reserved was left idle. In 1826 another Act was passed. The population of Oldham had nearly doubled in the interval, and the case therefore for reserving this land for recreation was very much more pressing. The promoters of the Bill recognized the fact of this increase, but they asked for, and obtained, an Act, not to make provision for recreation, but to enable the churchwardens and overseers to let this site for building land in aid of the rates, since Oldham "hath become very populous and is rapidly increasing in population."

At Gateshead 600 acres of Gateshead Fell were divided by an Act passed in 1809, without any allotment being made for any public purpose, except one acre for a church and churchyard. On the enclosure of a further 200 acres of commonable land in 1814, the Windmill Hills, an area of about 10 acres, were left open and vested in the borough holders and freemen. It was disputed later whether this land belonged to its holders as their private property, on which they could build houses, or was, as the Corporation argued, merely vested in them for the benefit of the public. Gateshead, meanwhile, was reported as being in great need of public walks. The question was not finally settled till 1861, when the borough holders handed over the ground to the Corporation, under a deed, with stipulations that it should be made an agreeable place of resort to the public.

Blackburn affords a case where the need for recreation was recognized in the early seventeenth century, but forgotten later. In 1618 the 1,266 acres of common and waste lands were enclosed and divided up amongst the owners of land in Blackburn, but some 18 acres were to be set out and used "for the mustering and training of people in that part, and for the recreation of the Inhabitants of the said Town, and for the good and profit of the said Town and Poor thereof, as a gift for ever. . . ." But when the Committee of 1833 held its enquiries, the rights of recreation had been lost.

Apart from deliberate inclosures, as towns grew, opportunities for recreation were restricted by the advance of building on land in private hands. Thus, in Birmingham, though there were no parks, no public open spaces, or common lands, yet in the early nineteenth century a considerable portion of the population had gardens of their own. ". . . It is the custom of Birmingham," said a witness in 1833, " for the working men to have gardens at about a guinea a year rent, of which there are a great number round the town, and all the better parts of the workmen spend their leisure hours there; a considerable portion of land in the immediate vicinity of Birmingham is let at £12 an acre for these small gardens." " Are they enabled," he was asked, " to go there with their children?" " Their children and families," was the answer, " they have little summer-houses, where they spend their evenings and Sundays." Nine years later it was reported that the gardens in which the mechanics " took great delight" were " now for the most part built over, and the mechanics of the town are gradually losing this source of useful and healthy recreation." The Spitalfields weavers suffered the same loss.

Nowhere was the neglect of any provision for exercise and open-air amusements more striking than in Manchester. The commons and wastes of the district had been, for the most part, early enclosed, and were now swamped by the tide of buildings. Newton Heath, a common or waste of 140 acres which survived through the eighteenth century, was enclosed in 1802. No provision was made on its enclosure for any recreation, but a liberal allotment was made in aid of the Poor Rates. " At present," wrote Dr. J. P. Kay in 1833, " the entire labouring population of Manchester is without any season of recreation, and is ignorant of all amusements, excepting that very small portion which frequents the theatre. Healthful exercise in the open air is seldom or never taken by the artisans of this town, and their health certainly suffers considerable depression from this deprivation. One reason of this state of the people is, that all scenes of interest are remote from the town, and that the walks which can be enjoyed by the poor are chiefly the turnpike roads, alternately dusty or muddy. Were parks provided, recreation would be taken with avidity, and one of the first results would be a better use of the Sunday, and a substitution of innocent amusement at all other times, for the debasing pleasures now in vogue. I need not inform you how sad is our labouring population here." Ten years later the position was unchanged. " With a teeming population," wrote Mr. Mott, " literally overflowing her boundaries, she has no public walks or resorts, either for the youthful or the adult portion of the community to snatch an hour's enjoyment." On one occasion, and one only, such institutional gardens as existed were opened to this melancholy population: " On the holiday given at Manchester in celebration of Her Majesty's marriage, extensive arrangements were made for holding a Chartist meeting, and for getting up what was called a demonstration of the working classes, which greatly alarmed the municipal magistrates. Sir Charles Shaw, the Chief Commissioner of Police, induced the mayor to get the Botanical Gardens, Zoological Gardens, and Museum of that town, and other institutions thrown open to the working classes at the hour they were urgently invited to attend the Chartist meeting. The mayor undertook to be personally answerable for any damage that occurred from throwing open the gardens and institutions to the classes who had never before entered them. The effect was that not more than two or three hundred people attended the political meeting, which entirely failed, and scarcely five shillings worth of damage was done in the gardens or in the public institutions by the workpeople, who were highly pleased. A further effect produced was, that the charges before the police of drunkenness and riot were on that day less than the average of cases on ordinary days."

Attempts were made from time to time in the House of Commons to save some common opportunities for enjoyment. Perhaps the most interesting was Peel's attempt to amend the Municipal Corporations Bill in Committee in 1835. In many towns there were common lands over which the privileged class of freemen had legal rights, which the public in some cases could use for recreation. When the Whigs brought in their measure for reforming the government of towns, Peel obtained the insertion of a clause which, had it survived, might have made considerable difference to the disposal of these lands.

Peel's view was " that most of the property of corporations was intended for the benefit of the community at large, and it would be desirable that the community should recover it as soon as possible." By long prescription it had been appropriated to the use of certain descriptions of inhabitants only, and it was now desirable that it should be put " into the hands of the commonalty as speedily as possible consistent with justice to the rights of individuals." The Whigs accepted Peel's view; but the House of Lords took out of the Bill the clauses that gave effect to it. The House of Commons was unhappily so much occupied with fighting the Lords on other points, that it accepted defeat on this.

The next move for the defence of public rights was made by Hume. On March 9, 1837, he proposed a resolution in the House of Commons " that in all Inclosure Bills provision be made for leaving an open space sufficient for the purposes of exercise and recreation of the neighbouring population." Peel, then leader of the Opposition, though doubtful about the actual form of the resolution, gave warm support to Hume's object. He pointed out, with truth, that the subject had been urged on the attention of the Legislature, but that the Legislature had refused to attend. He laid down a sound doctrine that though the people might have no legal right to portions of waste lands or commons "they had a moral right," and he urged that even where no enclosure took place it would be a "wise and prudent expenditure of public money" to give a grant of £5,000 or £10,000 to aid local authorities.

Hume's motion was passed. It was supplemented two years later by Harvey, who moved (April 9, 1839) a resolution, afterwards made into a standing order, that in all Enclosure Bills "provision be made for leaving an open space in the most appropriate situation sufficient for purposes of exercise and recreation of the neighbouring population," and that provision be made "for efficient fencing of the allotment." Harvey made a long speech about the iniquities of Enclosure Bills, and the small allowance made for recreation allotments, instancing 3 acres out of 1,300, or 10 to 20 out of 10,000. He suggested that there should be "a poor man's Commissioner" to see that a suitable reservation was made, and urged the House to protect the poor in view of the "spirit of the times and the symptoms moving around them."

The intentions of the House of Commons were good, but the actual allotments made under these standing orders were meagre. An illustration is afforded by the case of Bradford. Near Bradford there was an open space of from 20 to 30 acres called Fairweather Green. According to a witness before the 1840 Health of Towns Committee, this space was used for games by "the population for five and six miles round, it is the only place for the purpose in the whole neighbourhood."

But whilst this Committee was sitting, a private Bill was passing through Parliament, prepared by Mr. Lister, one of the largest proprietors concerned, to enclose this green and some other parcels of waste land, amounting in all to 170 acres. Mr. Joseph Ellison, the witness referred to, protested against the reservation in the Act of 3 acres only "as a Place of Exercise and Recreation for the neighbouring Population," a population that he estimated at 120,000. On Fairweather Green, he pointed out, it was the custom to play at cricket, and "a game we call spell and nur; they will drive a ball, 10, 11, 12, 13 and 14 score; they cannot play at those games in three acres."

An attempt on different lines was made by James Silk Buckingham, better known as a temperance reformer. Buckingham, who started life as a sailor, had been expelled from India for exposing abuses. He was elected for Sheffield in 1832, and sat in the House of Commons for five years. For three years in succession he introduced Bills to "facilitate the formation of and establishment of Public Walks, Playgrounds, Baths and Places of healthy Recreation and Amusement." He proposed that a public meeting, convened at the request of fifty ratepayers, should have the power to decide by a majority of two-thirds of the ratepayers present to establish places for recreation, and a committee elected for the purpose was to have the power to borrow up to ten shillings per head per inhabitant, and to levy a rate of not more than threepence in the pound to provide interest and to pay off the borrowed money in twenty years' time. Fundamental rules were laid down for the guidance of the local committees, including one "that the Play Grounds be adapted for Gymnastic Exercises, Cricket, Archery, and other healthy sports, but that all conflicts of a personally irritating nature, such as Wrestling, Cudgelling and

Boxing be prohibited, as well as all Games in which cruelty to Animals is involved." Buckingham was curiously sanguine when he introduced his first Public Walks Bill, together with a kindred Bill for providing Literary and Scientific Institutes and Museums. He expected, he said, no objection, and declared that " in the course of a very few years, if these Bills should pass into a law we shall see as many public walks, gardens, and pleasure grounds in the neighbourhood of all our towns, as are now to be found on the Continent of Europe." But apathy proved as effective as regular opposition. If one of his Bills managed to reach the Report stage, consideration of the Report was deferred again and again, and the session came to an end without further progress. It was not until 1847 that local authorities were allowed to use the rates for making a public park without obtaining a special Act. One of the clauses in the Towns Improvements Act contained this provision, and it was incorporated in the Public Health Act of the following year.

A study of the local papers shows how great a strain this life without playing fields or amenities of any kind put upon the English temperament. Towns pass laws to forbid children from playing with tops in the streets; correspondents write to complain of the flying of kites and magistrates impose severe fines on men and boys for running races on the turnpike roads on the ground that this practice has become a general nuisance. For the English taste for games is old and deeply rooted. Chamberlayne remarked on it in his book on England written in 1660. Our reputation abroad is illustrated by the epigram quoted by Madariaga describing the English character: " One Englishman a fool, two Englishmen a football match; three Englishmen the British Empire."

CHAPTER VI

RELIGION AND CULTURE

" One chief cause of the dislike which the labouring population entertain for religious services is thought to be the maintenance of those distinctions by which they are separated as a class from the class above them. Working men, it is contended, cannot enter our religious structures without having pressed upon their notice some memento of their inferiority. The existence of pews and the position of the free seats are, it is said, alone sufficient to deter them from our churches; and religion has thus come to be regarded as a purely middle-class propriety or luxury." Census of 1851, *Religious Worship in England and Wales*, abridged from the Official Report made by Horace Mann to George Graham, Registrar-General, p. xciv.

ABOUT the character of the Methodist revival, the most important event in eighteenth-century England, there is general agreement. It was one of the periodical outbursts of vitality that have marked the history of Christianity; for its predecessors we must turn to the great movements associated with such names as those of St. Benedict, St. Francis, John Wycliffe, and John Huss. Its founder created a body of preachers who resembled the early disciples of St. Francis, alike in their relation to the religion in power and in their view of their own mission. Their business was not to teach a new theology, but to bring ardour and purpose into a Church whose teaching had become formal and cold, and whose life and conduct reflected and respected too faithfully the spirit and outlook of the world. They were not rebels against the authority of this indolent and comfortable institution; they were rebels against the easy-going pagan life of the time, with its neglect of the passionate gospel which the Christian Church came to life to preach. The Church had become more like a school of social manners than a witness to a militant faith; there was no note of indignation or rapture in its pulpits. The Methodists desired to supply the fervour that was lacking. They were not Nonconformists but revivalists, and they succeeded in reviving both the Established and the Nonconformist Churches. The relation in which they stood to the Church was well illustrated by the rules that Wesley laid down forbidding preachers to hold services in Church hours unless the incumbent was a " notoriously wicked man " or unless he preached Arian or " equally pernicious doctrine."

These early preachers resembled the Franciscans in another respect. They practised an austere simplicity of life; they were to make themselves conspicuous amid the levity of the age by their earnest and solemn behaviour. A strict discipline was required of them. They were not to use tobacco for " smoaking, chewing, or snuff," except on doctor's orders; they were to fast; they were to avoid spirituous liquors; they were " to converse sparingly and cautiously with women, particularly with young women "; preachers desiring to marry were to consult their brethren, and any member who married an unbeliever was to be expelled. They were bidden expressly not to affect the gentleman, but to remember that a preacher of the Gospel is the servant of all.

Religion has been defined by Professor Whitehead as " what a man does with his solitariness," and in this sense it may be as self-regarding as any other activity. It may take a man no further than his own shadow. For it may take him from his material cares and ambitions to plunge him in meditations in which his own life in a different aspect is still the centre. " Methodism with its eye forever turned on its own navel; asking itself with torturing anxiety of Hope and Fear, ' Am I right? am I wrong? Shall I be saved? shall I not be damned? '—what is this," asked Carlyle, " at bottom, but a new phasis of *Egoism*, stretched out into the Infinite? not always the heavenlier for its infinitude! " Carlyle's description was true of one kind of Methodist. But of course a man may do with his solitariness something nobler than this. The chapels, if they found a home for men and women tormented by such anxieties, found a home also for men and women in whose passionate desire for communion with God " the unseen took shape to common eye." In this way religion made numbers of men and women happier, more unselfish, more ready to pity the sorrows of their fellow men, more ready to undertake burdens for their relief. The Methodist movement did for eighteenth-century England what Christianity did for the ancient world, giving to men of conscience and compassion a cause for which to live, and blending the idea of the brotherhood of man with the most sublime of the mysteries of religion.

There is, however, a sense in which religion is not what a man does with his solitariness, but what a man does with his gregariousness. Religion gave its colour to the collective imagination of the primitive village watching anxiously the seasons of sowing and harvest. Sometimes in the history of the world it has almost filled the content of that imagination. You could not say of Churchmen or Methodists or Baptists that they were merely so many men and women worshipping in their own way without any common life or any common influence. " Christianity is first of all a way of life in fellowship." Fellowship takes a man out of his solitariness. These religious bodies were not only bodies of men holding certain beliefs and practising religious observances; they were bodies of people with a discipline affecting social conduct.

A moral revolt is always apt to answer extravagance by extravagance. The Methodist revolt was no exception. It was a revolt against dissolute manners, and it demanded ascetic manners. Wesley was proud, it will be remembered, that the Methodists abstained from "reading plays, romances, or books of humour, from singing innocent songs, or talking in a gay diverting manner." He said that to educate a child you must break his will, and when he drew up the rules for his school at Kingswood he said that he allowed no time for play, because he who plays as a boy will play when he is a man. If a man puts play outside his life, he surrenders tastes and pleasures that are an essential part of human history: the source of much of the beauty, the grace, the power, and the virtue, that distinguish higher from lower forms of character and intelligence. A man or a society may make that sacrifice for a particular object. And a man who has renounced something, taking stern vows upon himself, at the bidding of conscience, is richer as well as poorer. For an ascetic life touches the imagination of the man who chooses it, since deliberate sacrifice is an act of resolution, bringing the satisfaction that comes from living your life at a bracing pitch. But to serve this purpose an ascetic life must be the choice of the man who leads it. When an ascetic life is thrust on others, it deprives them of opportunities for satisfying their imagination in which mankind has found light and inspiration, and puts nothing in their place.

The influence of this spirit, spread over the life of the time, was manifest in the decline of the theatre. The

last half of the eighteenth century has been described by
Lecky as the golden age of the English drama: "It saw
Garrick, Macklin, and Barry in their prime; it witnessed
the splendid rise of John Kemble and Mrs. Siddons, as
well as the lighter graces of Miss Farren, Mrs. Jordan,
and Mrs. Abington, and at a time when the great Shake-
spearean revival was at its height, it also produced the
plays of Goldsmith, Sheridan, Foote, and Home. There
was an incontestable improvement in the moral tendency,
and still more in the refinement of the theatre, and it was
noticed that a coarseness which excited no reprobation
under George I was no longer tolerated on the stage.
The revolt of popular feeling against the legislative
discouragement of the theatre had now become very
marked." This revolt showed itself in the evasion of the
Act of 1737, which had confined the legitimate drama to
the Haymarket, Covent Garden, and Drury Lane, and
also in the money spent by the large towns to obtain a
special Act of Parliament to enable them to set up a
theatre. In this way theatres were provided between
1767 and 1775 in Edinburgh, Bath, Bristol, York, Hull,
Liverpool, Manchester, and Chester. In 1778 a conces-
sion was made, and magistrates were allowed to grant
licences for special performances for sixty days. Tate
Wilkinson, an actor, took companies to the North of
England, where good plays were given, either in Theatres
Royal set up by special Act of Parliament, or in theatres
licensed on this plan. Mrs. Siddons, Mrs. Jordan, and
other good actors visited the provinces every year.

If anybody had been told in 1780 that in the next half-
century the English people would grow much richer; that
the picture given in his book by Tate Wilkinson, of the
country gentlemen round Wakefield who supported his
theatre there, would seem modest in comparison with the

wealth that would spring up round all the new towns; that every industrial town would have a large, comfortable class with leisure; that this accession of wealth would be accompanied by a burst of literary power; he might well have supposed that the theatre would play a great part in the life of this time, and help to guide and inspire the imagination of the great population whose fortunes have been followed in these pages. What would have seemed more natural than that writers who were masters of another literary form, like Scott and Dickens, would turn to the drama, as Fielding and Goldsmith had turned to it in the eighteenth century, and as Galsworthy and Bennett were to turn to it in the twentieth; that Dickens, who was to do more to draw English people together than any other influence in the time, would write comedies, as he wrote novels, that rich and poor alike could enjoy? What would have been the surprise of such a person to be told that the theatre would rapidly decline, that in 1853 there would be one theatre in Manchester and no theatre at all in Salford, and that in 1873 Kingsley would be able to write, "Few highly educated men now think it worth while to go to see any play, and that exactly for the same reasons as the Puritans put forward; and still fewer highly educated men think it worth while to write plays; finding that since the grosser excitements of the imagination have become forbidden themes, there is really very little to write about."

There were, of course, more causes than one for this remarkable decline. The law was still adverse in certain ways. Down to 1834 dramatic authors had no protection, and provincial theatres could act a piece that had been given in London, without paying the author anything. It was not until 1843 that magistrates were allowed to license theatres. More general reasons are to be found

in the rise of the cheap print and rival attractions. But
undoubtedly one cause was the influence of the Methodists. That influence was exerted with some success even
in the early days of Methodism. In 1764 John Wesley
wrote to the Mayor and Corporation of Bristol protesting
against the proposal to build a theatre, not merely
because " most of the present stage entertainments sap
the foundation of all religion," but also because a theatre
would be " peculiarly hurtful to a trading city, giving a
wrong turn to youth especially, gay, trifling, and directly
opposite to the spirit of industry and close application to
business." He added that the Corporation of Nottingham had been led by these considerations to forbid the
building of a new theatre. Wesley was using here an
argument that served for men who were not Methodists.
Thus Archbishop Cornwallis—not much of a Methodist
in his own habits, for his Sunday parties at Lambeth
drew down a rebuke from George III—opposed the
Manchester Playhouse Bill in 1775 on the ground that
theatres encouraged idleness in industrial towns. Tate
Wilkinson had to encounter strong opposition in the
provinces, and he described the outbursts of a clergyman
of the Low Church at Hull, who declared that " everyone
who entered a playhouse was, with the players, equally
certain of eternal damnation." As Methodism spread
among the employing class, this influence spread in the
industrial towns. Dickens deplored the effect in discouraging the theatre and encouraging less desirable sub-
stitutes. Three months before his death he wrote that
" the narrow-minded fanatics who decry the theatre and
defame its artists are absolutely the advocates of depraved
and barbarous amusements. For wherever a good drama
and well-regulated theatre decline, some distorted form
of theatrical entertainment will inevitably arise in their

place." He pointed out that this moral had been urged in *Hard Times*.

The Methodists did with the English Sunday what they did with the English theatre. For the mass of the working classes there was only one day on which they were free from the discipline of mill and workshop. On that day they were refused recreation for mind or body, music or games, beauty of art or nature. They sought diversions where they could find them. The Yorkshire and Lancashire papers are full of complaints that the youth of the large towns spent Sunday gambling in the streets, or in drunkenness and brutal sports, and that the behaviour of the populace was distressing and inconvenient to respectable people. An engineer who had been abroad described the difference in this respect between English and Continental life. He told the Factory Commission that at Mülhausen, where most of the people were Protestant, the workmen went to church in the morning and spent the rest of the day in the country playing games, whereas in England " a man can do nothing but go to a public house on Sunday, and when there you can do nothing but drink." Chadwick, who cited the engineer's evidence, suggested to the Committee on Drunkenness that public gardens should be provided, with free admission after morning service on Sundays. Unhappily Sabbatarian prejudice was too strong, and the English people were left to gloom and drink.

The fate of the Botanical Gardens at Leeds is a good illustration of the strength of this Puritan feeling. The Gardens did not pay, and when the shareholders decided to give them up, it was proposed that the town council should acquire them. The *Leeds Intelligencer* gave strong support to this proposal, suggesting that they should be thrown open on Sundays, as that was the only day when the working classes could enjoy them. This was too bold a plan for respectable Leeds, whose scruples were well represented in a leading article that was published a few months later in the *Leeds Mercury* on the subject of Sabbath observance. "It would be a wretched exchange to draw the poor of England out of their Churches, Chapels, Sunday-schools and quiet homes into public exhibitions and places of amusement on the Lord's Day." The "quiet homes" in which the poor of Leeds were invited to spend their happy Sundays included a good many houses of the kind described by Mr. Robert Baker in his Sanitary Report, where fourteen people lay ill of typhus, without a single bed in the place.

Leeds was not peculiar in this respect. At Liverpool we read, "on Sundays . . . all the public houses are opened, and all the public walks, cemeteries and zoological and botanical gardens, where the people might amuse themselves innocently, are closed." "Have the public a right of going to those gardens on any day?"— "Not the public generally; but the cemeteries are opened to the public every day of the week except Sunday." Manchester was under the same cloud. The *North of England Magazine* published a series of sketches describing the life of that city in 1842, and the shutting of the Zoological Gardens on Sundays was cited as one of the worst injustices inflicted on the mass of the population. The writer quoted a French observer Bruet, who remarked, "The observance of the Sunday in England is rigorously enforced by church and state. There is only one exception: the dram shops. All shops must be closed, all places of innocent amusement or instruction, such as Botanical Gardens or Museums, must be rigorously shut, but the folding doors of the gin palace may open to any man who pushes his foot against them."

F. D. Maurice reminded these strict Sabbatarians who were afraid of the counter-attraction of "a few statues and a few gardens," that the Christian religion had made its way in the Roman Empire against theatre and amphi-theatre and ample facilities for gratifying every intel-lectual and every brutal taste. Maurice's comparison takes us back to the topics of the early chapters of this book. Everybody knows that Christianity put its ban on the brutal amusements there described, forbidding Christians the vulgar and sensual pleasures of the theatre and the brutal and bloody pleasures of the arena. One incident of the long struggle between the old habits and the new morality has made a lasting mark on the memory of mankind. In 404 A.D. the monk Telemachus threw himself into the arena, and by his dramatic death brought to an end the gladiators' combats which for six centuries had delighted and degraded the Roman mind.

But Christianity was not in this sphere of common enjoyment merely a repressive and negative influence. It came in time to use and stimulate æsthetic tastes and impulses, substituting for the spectacles that excited the emotions by horror those that excited the emotions by splendour. "In the Middle Ages," says Powicke, "the hold of the Church was due to the fact that it could satisfy the best cravings of the whole man, his love of beauty, his desire for goodness, his endeavour after truth." Even in the dark ages, amid all the disorder and violence of the sixth century, the love of beauty found satisfaction in the ritual of the Church. Dill, in his picture of Gaul in the Merovingian Age, describes the magnificent pomp of the Christian ceremonies. "Perhaps the one bright moment for the peasant amid days of toil was the hour in church, with stately processions in vari-coloured vestments, advancing to the sound of rhythmic chants, through aisles hung with rich tapestries, and decorated with brilliant frescoes and marbles, to the sanctuary gleaming with the radiance of jewels on the Cross." He quotes a writer of the time who said, " Ad nova templa avide concurrunt undique plebes." And for the peasants, suffering every kind of injustice in this world of violence and oppression, as for Clovis who declared as he listened to the story of the Crucifixion that could he have been there with his Franks he would have avenged it, the new religion provided some satisfaction for the spirit that could enjoy tragedy under the Greeks and cruelty under the Romans. " We may imagine," says Dill, " the effect of a choir at Rheims or Tours chanting, with all the fury and the conscious power of a Church which held the keys of Hell, the words ' Fiant filii orphani et uxor ejus vidua; deleatur nomen ejus et dispereat de terra memoria eorum; qui insurgunt in me confundantur.' "

What effort did the Methodists who imposed the ascetic habits of the Bleak Age make themselves to satisfy the imagination of the working classes? They were confronted with a great population of uneducated men and women, who had lost that touch with nature which is the inspiration of all religion, living in surroundings where nothing bore witness to the gracious or the solemn beauty of the world. The daily struggle for a livelihood was made harsher and more absorbing, because the prestige of power and wealth was unchallenged, and self-respect and poverty seemed incompatible. The mill to-day; the workhouse to-morrow. To minds caught and held in this inexorable rhythm, religion could only speak by an impressive symbolism, by beauty of building or music. Did the Methodism that put a ban on the social life and culture of the eighteenth century, in the name of religion, substitute the culture of the Middle Ages, when religion had drawn into its own service, and used for its own dignity, the arts by which the Greeks had given to their drama its solemn power?

The Methodists made one notable contribution. By a happy fortune the two Wesleys were poets and musicians, and singing became an important feature of Methodist services. Wesley published a book of hymns and tunes, " designed chiefly for the use of the people called Methodist," and in his *Journal* he described from time to time the pleasure with which he had noticed the progress of music. In 1787 he found a Sunday School at Bolton, with eight hundred children, of whom a hundred were taught singing. He was disturbed by a tendency in some places to introduce more formal music, and he drew up rules for the guidance of chapels. Anthems were not to be sung; great care was to be taken in training; and the whole congregation was to be exhorted to sing, " not one in ten only." Coleridge said that the hearty congregational singing of English hymns kept the Methodists together, and Horace Mann, when commenting on the figures of the Religious Census, said that the Methodists had discovered a form of service specially suitable for poor people.

With this exception, music played little part in the religious life of the time. Wesley, fearing quarrels over the introduction of organs, said that no organ was to be placed in a chapel until it was proposed in Conference. One of the fiercest controversies in the Methodist world arose over a conflict at Brunswick Street Chapel, Leeds, in 1828, on this question. A later writer remarked that at this time poor men and women in the Yorkshire towns used to save up their pennies for an oratorio, and yet religious bodies were very slow to satisfy this desire in public worship. Bishop Blomfield deprecated the introduction of cathedral services, the use of surplices, and processions, and when a clergyman wrote describing the ordinary church services as " blank, dismal, oppressive, and dreary," he replied, " If the minister *reads* with devotion and solemnity (not *intones*); if the congregation join in the responses and psalmody; and if sound doctrine and practical exhortations be earnestly and affectionately delivered by the preacher, such epithets as you have used are grievously misapplied." Raumer suggested that the utter want of all musical education for the people was a result of the way in which Sunday was observed.

Religion was thus making little use of the arts. The new chapels were bare and ugly; music made its way slowly and with difficulty; there were few imposing ceremonies in church; no rich and noble pageants in the streets, to bring history into the life of Hunslet or Ancoats. Satisfaction was found for the starved dramatic sense of the age in the rhetoric, so common then in church and chapel, which painted the torments of everlasting fire. It is significant that the biographer of the famous Methodist preacher, William Dawson, speaking of his power as a pulpit orator, chose his handling of this topic as the best example of his gifts. Dawson told his terrified hearers that a man's torment in hell would be all the fiercer because his parents had prayed for him. This stern and forbidding Sunday, with its sanctions of childish terror, its " codes of fearful fantasy," was the gift of religion to a people needing above all things some space in its life in which it could lose itself in noble wonder, in the enjoyment of beauty of form or sound, in submission to ideas that could stir the spirit of fellowship and communion. " The lower classes," said Raumer, " who often have to toil wearily through every other day, find Sunday as it is constantly described, the weariest of all. Often after serving an austere master, they are made to find in the Father of Love, an austerer still."

There is another aspect in which this comparison with early Christianity bears on the theme of this book. If the Church substituted in course of time its own spectacles for those of the theatre, replacing the excitement of the arena by the display of vestment and ritual, this was not its only, or its first, or its chief, contribution to the social regeneration of the Roman world. The most striking quality in the early Church, the Church of the first three centuries from which Augustine drew his picture of the City of God, is described in Toynbee's phrase, " a rival civilization of the proletariate." In the dialogue written by Minucius Felix, a writer of the second century A.D., the pagan Caecilius is made to reproach Christianity with collecting the dregs of the people, and the Christian Octavius replies that this is not a reproach but a glory. Murray and Tarn have shown how widespread was the discontent of the submerged world before the advent of Christianity, and how ardently men were dreaming of equality and fellowship. " The first Utopia, Zeno's," says Tarn, " was too splendid and remote for human nature to grasp. But Euhemerus (C. 300) and Iambulus (third century) created true modern Utopias, located on islands in the Indian Ocean, and in Iambulus' great Sun-state Stoic communism appears full grown." When Aristonicus of Pergamum raised a revolt against Rome in 132 B.C., he and the Stoic Blossius preached these ideas, and their motley army destroyed a Roman Consul and his legions. Early Christian churches gave effect to these revolutionary ideas in their daily life and practice, abolishing not merely in the dreams of philosophers, but, before the eyes of men, the distinctions between rich and poor, bond and free, bringing, as Tarn puts it, to those who laboured and were heavy laden, a different hope from any that Hellenism could offer.

In the bleak age there was ample room for this kind of Christianity, but the Established Church and the Methodists alike were hampered by their difficulties from playing this part in the life of the new proletariate.

The difficulty of the Church was plain enough on the surface. Early Christianity ceased to be a rival civilization of the proletariate when it was taken into partnership by the Empire. It gained recognition from the state but lost the simplicity that had given it its moral power over the poor. The English Church resembled not the early Church, but the Church that had been accepted and established by Constantine. At the time of the Reform Bill the English Church was part of an aristocratic system of government, corrupted like every other part of that system by the abuses that come when the sense of possession is stronger than the sense of duty. The Church was regarded, like the pocket boroughs, as a great system of patronage and property at the disposition of the richer classes.

Parsons could hold several livings together, putting curates, who were paid in some instances like the poorest labourers, in the less desirable and less healthy parishes. In 1810 there were 6,000 livings in which the incumbent was non-resident. Hay, the Vicar of Rochdale, one of the richest livings in England, was non-resident most of the time. Even as late as 1838 there were over 4,000 non-resident parsons. Chapters were as greedy and as ruthless as individuals. A Dean and Chapter would take £1,000 or £2,000 from a parish and pay somebody like Parson Andrewes to do the work £50 a year, or even less. The Church thus combined in its ranks men with princely incomes for which some of them rendered no service at all, and curates who were as badly off as the village labourer who was driven to live on the Speenhamland dole. With a Church so governed and inspired there was, of course, no relation between spiritual needs and the ministrations of the Church. There was not a single bishop in Lancashire or the West Riding until 1836. Churches were, like members of Parliament, most numerous where least needed.

Soon after the passing of the Reform Bill these sensational abuses were removed, partly by the influence of reformers within the Church, partly by legislation initiated by Peel and carried on by Russell. An organ for internal reform was set up in the Ecclesiastical Commission; scandals disappeared: attempts were made to supply the neglected districts by new bishoprics at Manchester and Ripon; the glaring inequality between the incomes of different sees was removed; members of Chapters were forbidden to hold more than one benefice or to belong to more than one Chapter, and it was made illegal to hold two benefices if they were more than a mile apart, or if the additional stipend exceeded £1,000.

With these reforms there disappeared the resounding scandals that had filled so many sparkling pages in the Radical pamphlets of the time. Cobbett's *Legacy to Parsons* was now a book for the library shelf rather than the political platform; a stern hand had been laid on the corruption which had displayed so splendid a target for his incomparable invective. This was a great achievement, but it would be false to say of it that it had solved the urgent problem that faced the Church. It was one thing to put an end to sinecures and abuses and to give a serious and responsible character to the office of its parsons, hitherto regarded and held with such levity; it was another to satisfy the imagination of the great population on whose daily life of bleak and monotonous toil those civilizing influences to which mankind has looked for comfort, ever since the first city found shelter behind its circling walls, shed so pale and doubtful a light. How far could the Church succeed in helping men and women to turn away from the hard face of a struggle, in which wealth brought fame, and poverty contempt, to this mysterious atmosphere, where the soul of Dives was no more esteemed than the soul of Lazarus? The importance of religion, like the importance of culture, or the importance of beauty, in the social setting examined in these pages, depended on its power to create a world of its own, with standards, duties, and satisfactions other than those set and sought in the race for wealth.

The difficulties of the Church were summed up in a sentence by Bishop Blomfield when he was giving evidence before the Committee on the Observance of the Sabbath, in 1832: " It is the object of the Commissioners for building new churches, as far as they can, to intermingle the seats of the rich and the poor, so as to afford the latter nearly the same facilities for hearing which the former enjoy. We have found considerable difficulty in realizing our own wishes in that respect, on account of the objections which were made by the richer classes to too great an intermixture of the poor among them, objections which it was absolutely necessary to attend to because the whole income of the Minister depends on the pew rents accruing exclusively from the richer classes."

Hook's achievement at Leeds shows that the difficulties that faced the Church were not insuperable to a man with a genius for leadership. When he went to Leeds in

1838 the Church was hated by the Dissenters and ignored by everybody else. There were fifty communicants. The parishioners, who elected seven out of the eight church-wardens, used to elect a standing opposition to the Vicar, who appointed the eighth. Hook was vicar for twenty-eight years. When he left, the Church was a power in Leeds as nowhere else in England for he had converted a Church despised and disliked into a Church that inspired affection and respect among all classes. Blomfield had explained that the wishes of the rich Church-men had to be considered in manufacturing districts. Hook never acted on this principle. He told the squires and farmers at a great agricultural dinner at Leeds, that one of the first needs of the time was to give the agricultural labourer leisure and education. He took the chair on several occasions at meetings in favour of the Ten Hours Bill, even when the principal speaker was so tempestuous an orator as Oastler. He lost subscriptions for his churches in consequence, for he had just issued his manifesto to the people of Leeds, and the Evangelicals were seeking to stir up opposition among the rich. In his early days at Leeds the Chartists ran a list of candidates at the meeting for electing churchwardens, and carried all of them. The Chartist churchwardens who were thus thrust upon Hook soon learned to respect him: they worked with him and not against him, and one of them became an ardent churchman. Workmen helped to administer all his organizations, and to provide funds for his schemes. Thirteen churches were built and the parish church rebuilt while he was vicar, but he had no difficulty in raising the money needed for his parishes, and Church rates were never imposed. Two incidents illustrate the confidence and esteem which he inspired among the poorer classes. When the Queen visited Leeds, the Friendly Societies chose him to present their address of welcome; during a strike in the mining industry, the colliers asked for arbitration by three arbitrators, one to be named by the employers, one by the men, and the third by the Vicar of Leeds.

Hook's career shows what could be done by a man of character and power. But it illustrates also another aspect of the Church's difficulties. The Church was distracted between the two movements which had brought power and purpose into its life. The Evangelical movement had brought earnestness and devotion; the Tractarian movement had brought a wider and deeper sense of the place of religion in history and civilization. The great change in the character and spirit of the clergy which is apparent if we contrast 1850 with 1800 is the result largely of these two movements. But the movements were rivals, and bitter rivals, and at this time they were chiefly occupied with their controversies. Hook suffered at the hands of both schools, Evangelicals and Puseyites alike putting difficulties in his way. The Church which had to overtake the neglect of half a century was thus disabled and distracted by its internal conflicts. Dr. Gore has remarked that after the third century the emphasis in the history of the Christian Church passed from right living to right thinking, from conduct to orthodoxy. Something like this happened in early Victorian England. The Church was full of vitality and movement, rich in thinkers, teachers, men of saintly life and serious scholarships. Newman, Pusey, Maurice, Robertson and Whateley were all helping to form the English mind of the next generation, but in the days when Chartism was spreading over the towns this intellectual vigour found its expression in the bitter strife of Evangelical and Tractarian. " The conviction has been

brought home to some of us with terrible force," wrote
F. D. Maurice, " that while religious men are disputing
. . . the great body of Englishmen is becoming bitterly
indifferent to us all and smiles grimly and contemptu-
ously at our controversies." While the party men led by
Pusey and Shaftesbury, " theological champions armed at
all points," were filling the Church with the sound of
conflict, the mass of the poor in most of the great towns
remained outside it.

Methodism, like the Church, had its difficulties, the
difficulties that are brought by success. In the eighteenth
century Methodism was in its spirit more like the early
Church than the Church as it became under Constantine's
aegis. It won its greatest triumphs among the poor.
Wesley and his disciples converted whole districts like
the mining parts of Cornwall from a life of dissipation
and plunder to devout and orderly habits. All over
England and Wales great numbers of ignorant men and
women were brought for the first time under religion's
spell.

In some parts of England and Wales Methodism was
still a Revivalist movement in the forties. Thus the
Commission on the Employment of Children in 1843
gave a glowing account of the work done by the Methodists in districts like the Forest of Dean and North Wales,
closely resembling the descriptions of Wesley's work in
Cornwall. The colliers had been the terror of the sur-
rounding country " for gross ignorance, rudeness, and
irreligion, almost without parallel in any Christian community." Churches there were none except on the
extreme outskirts; the great area of the Forest being
extra-parochial, though very populous, and schools were
almost unknown. In this district a striking change had
been produced by the work of the Dissenters. " The

success of their zeal is everywhere exhibited in the immense number of chapels which have been built within the last thirty years. The money to build them has been drawn from the pockets of the farmers, small tradesmen, and the working orders, by means of penny subscriptions in the chapels, to which even the boys who are earning wages contribute." So in North Wales: "What the established Church has not yet been able to supply, the Dissenters have; chapels have everywhere been built by them, and their efforts, always unsupported and often scoffed at by the clergy, gentry, and influential proprietors, have been attended with signal success."

In many industrial districts, on the other hand, Methodism was rather one of the settled religions than a new and passionate gospel. It was no longer despised or persecuted, but it was no longer a religion of the proletariate. Horace Mann, who drew up the Report on the Religious Census of 1851, said that most of the new chapels had been built for the middle classes, and that as the towns separated into respectable and proletarian districts, the poor were worse off in this respect as in others. The Irish immigrants probably suffered less, for they had their Catholic chapels and priests in their midst, and it is significant that in the cholera epidemics the deaths of Catholic priests are often noted in the papers. Faucher said that he did not see the working classes in the chapels of Manchester and Leeds. The people walking along the streets belonged exclusively to the middle classes. The operatives loitered at their doors or lounged at street corners until the hour of service was over and the public houses open. Methodism, in losing its first missionary character, had fallen to some extent under the shadow of respectability. In early days the weavers used to attend chapel with their aprons rolled round their waists, and some of them had thought that to drop their aprons would mean that they had conformed to the world. These democratic habits had disappeared. In 1842 the Annual Report of the Wesleyan Methodist Conference regretted that in times of distress the poor neglected chapel "because a want of suitable clothing leaves a meanness in their appearance which is chiefly conspicuous for its being contrasted with that of the more favoured of their brethren." A witness before the Health of Towns Commission drew the line between those who could dress for chapel and those who could not. "The general practice is, on the Sunday evening for those who are not able to make a decent appearance at a place of worship to congregate together, pay their halfpenny or penny, and send for a newspaper from a public-house."

The distinction between the respectable and the common people was emphasized in chapel as in church, by the distinction between pews and free seats. This distinction had brought with it all the dangers that Wesley dreaded, for Wesley had stood out against the system of pew rents. In Wesley's London headquarters, the Foundry, "all benches were alike. No difference was made here between the rich and the poor; no one was allowed to call any seat his own, first comers sat down first." In December 1787 Wesley had a difference with his Committee on this point, and his language shows what a serious view he took of the threatened change. "The Committee proposed to me . . . that everyone who took a pew should have it as his own. Thus over-turning, at one blow, the discipline which I had been establishing for fifty years." Three days later he reports the satisfactory result of the discussion. "We had another meeting of the Committee, who after a calm and loving consultation, judged it best that none should claim any pew of his own, either in the new chapel or in West Street." But Wesley's principle did not long survive him.

"Our chapels," wrote a leading Wesleyan minister in the *Watchman* in 1849, "have been fitted up too much as private dwellings than as places of public worship; and the free sittings, if sufficient, not made readily perceivable nor easily accessible. I could name chapels with expensive architectural frontispieces of stone and with interior ornaments of ' dead white and gold ' where the poor's seats are like sheep pens, in the four corners of the building and behind the pulpit; and where, even then, the seats adjoining are screened off most carefully by high rods and curtains. I am no believer in the doctrine of ' equality ' as it is now expounded by many— I regard it as foolish and contrary to the order of God. . . . But admitting all this, it is not only unbecoming but detrimental to Methodism (and it would be so to any church) thus to appear to neglect the poor."

Early in his career Wesley had been concerned for the future of Methodism. "I do not see," he wrote in 1787, "how it is possible in the nature of things for any revival of religion to continue long. For religion must necessarily produce both Industry and Frugality and these cannot but produce Riches. But as Riches increase so will Pride, Anger and Love of the World in all its branches." Nobody could deny that so far as the influence of Methodism in the great towns was concerned, Wesley's fears had come true. Halévy in its brilliant study described Puritan Nonconformity as " a stage in the history of the English family. The unskilled labourer becomes in turn a skilled workman, an artisan, the head of a small business, a business man possessed of a modest capital, and as he rises out of the barbarism in which the

working class was plunged, he becomes a Nonconformist."
Methodists made industrious and successful workmen,
tradesmen, managers and employers. It was natural for
men in this atmosphere to think that poverty was the
consequence of wickedness. A leading Nonconformist,
giving evidence on Church rates, remarked "Religion
always tends to give a man the power to pay for his
religion and the will." One of Galsworthy's characters
says much the same in the Skin Game, "God helps those
who help themselves, that is at the bottom of all religion."
As Methodism became a settled system it tended to take
rather than give a standard. The spirit of the age put
its bias and character on Methodism as on everything
else. The rich man of the Bible, who found it so difficult
to enter the Kingdom of Heaven, had been succeeded by
the rich man of the Puritan revival who stepped into
wealth and Paradise from the same ladder. For the rich
man was no longer the idle man, who enjoyed himself
while others toiled; he was the industrious man who made
others richer by his industry. Thus success and failure,
achievement and defeat, had come to look very much the
same inside and outside the chapel. If somebody had
said to a prosperous Methodist of Manchester or Leeds,
as Caecilius had said to Octavius, that his religion
collected the dregs of the people, the Methodist would
have considered it not a glory but a reproach.

CHAPTER VII

EDUCATION

THIS new world so cold to common pleasure might have been expected to look with special favour on common education. For, if we take the two opposing philosophies of the time, we see that they were in principle agreed on its importance. The fundamental philosophy underlying the humanist protest against the gospel of the Industrial Revolution—the idea that man was a complex character, and society a complex body, not to be left to the steam-engine and the railways for the satisfaction of instincts and tastes that had created and demanded, in other ages, art, culture, and religion—this idea, which inspired, in different forms, the teaching of Wordsworth and Mill, Coleridge and Carlyle, gave great importance to education as a national need. But the same conclusion was reached by the school that simplified human nature, taking individual opportunity for its watchword, looking to the incentive of gain as the moving power. For this school, as we have seen, did not consider that existing institutions gave full scope to the virtues of the economic system. "Remove all obstacles," they would have said, "to the spirit of initiative and enterprise, if you would see what the Industrial Revolution can do towards giving you a rich people instead of a poor people: a happy instead of a discontented people. Encourage thrift; abolish abuses in State, Church, and law; get rid of the Corn Laws which check the flow of exchange; spread education. Men may by force of genius make their way without education, but, if the principle of your social life is to be universal opportunity, universal education is essential." Thus, if education was demanded by Carlyle, who said "That a man should die ignorant, who had the capacity for knowledge —this to me is tragedy," it was also demanded by those who have said, "That a man should die poor, who had the capacity for wealth—this to me is tragedy." Men who differed on almost every other question agreed on this.

Unhappily the effect of this agreement was destroyed by another influence, the religious discord of the time. Religious controversy has not always been mischievous. The quarrels of the seventeenth century did good as well as harm. If they made the English people more combative and more intolerant, they made it also more democratic and more vigorous. Writers like Gooch, Laski and Lindsay, describing the rise of the Independents and the Baptists, trace to the revolt against control the religious vitality, and the sharp and stern sense of personal obligation which gave spiritual power to democratic ideas and democratic institutions in England. But of the religious quarrels of the forties, the feuds of Church and Chapel, of Catholic and Protestant, of High Church and Low Church, the mischief clearly outbalanced the advantages. "Such was the mild spirit of antiquity," said Gibbon in a famous passage, "that the nations were less attentive to the differences than to the resemblances of their religious worship." There was more religious strife in Manchester or Bradford in the forties than in the Roman Empire under the rule of Augustus.

A study of the struggle over this question reveals two

sources of difficulty; one the mischief done by these quarrels, the other, the mischief done by the false and limited view of education that was in fashion. Mill has described in a famous passage in his Autobiography the nervous breakdown that he suffered in consequence of the intensive education he received from his father, an education in which feeling was entirely neglected and the æsthetic impulses were starved or repressed. Mill's distress was really the distress of the age, and the mechanical method—the view as Newman put it that the printing press could do with mind what the steam engine had done with matter—was applied to popular education in fantastic forms. This becomes clear when we look into the character of the popular education that was given and the arrangements for giving it.

In 1834 the passion for social improvement and for accurate information induced a body of gentlemen in Manchester, who had formed a Statistical Society, to start an inquiry into the state of education in that town. The inquiry spread to neighbouring towns, to Salford, Liverpool, Bury, Bolton, Ashton, Dukinfield, Stalybridge, and even to York. Later, Birmingham and Bristol were also investigated in the same way. The results were digested and published in different reports, mostly between 1834 and 1837, and, from the remarks of the investigators, even more than from the numerous statistical tables, it is possible to form some estimate of the opportunities for schooling at that time. There was no compulsory attendance except for children working in factories, and there the schooling existed chiefly on paper.

Let us suppose that the parents of a small intelligent boy in Manchester, of what we should now call school age, were anxious that he should learn his letters and whatever else he could pick up. In 84 out of the 86

Sunday-schools in Manchester, he would be taught to read after a fashion, and in 10 of those schools he might learn writing too, but the process would be long and tedious, and we will suppose that his parents wished for instruction on week days. He would first be sent to one of the many Dame Schools scattered about the town (there were 230 of them in Manchester), where reading, and, for girls, sewing, were taught. If he were lucky he would live close to one of the old-fashioned type, where a tidy old lady would teach habits of neatness, even though her literary standards were not high. If he were very fortunate he would find himself at the school " kept by a blind man who hears his scholars their lessons and explains them with great simplicity." The blind teacher was liable to be interrupted by being called to turn his wife's mangle, but probably the lessons were none the worse for that. If he were less fortunate he would find that the Dame School was a dirty, close room, where children were sent not so much to learn as " to be taken care of and to be out of the way at home,"—" If I can keep a bit of quietness," said one of the Dames, " it is as much as I can do and as much as I am paid for "—where books to read and fresh air to breathe were equally scarce, where discipline depended on the rod, where the only saving grace was a certain slackness so that in hot weather, for instance, the children could stretch out their limbs (provided there were room) on forms or floor, and sleep away the weary afternoon. As a Bury mistress remarked with truth, by way of apology, " they were better so than awake." For the privilege of sending a child to one of these Dame Schools parents paid as a rule 4d. a week, some more, some less. The average income of the Manchester Dames was calculated to be £17, 16s. or 6s. 10d. a week, in Bury it was put at £19 a year. It was supple-

D

mented by earnings from other sources such as shop-
keeping, sewing, or washing. Teaching might be combined with keeping a cake shop, for which the pupils
provided a clientele, or with selling milk, in which case
the scholars could amuse themselves with dabbling in
the cans. Occasionally the poor rates provided the necessary supplement, but this was rare.

In his next stage the boy would go to what the Statistical Society called a " Common Day School," that is a
school kept by a master or mistress who made his or her
living by it. This was the type of school at which the
majority of boys and girls in Manchester obtained their
education, such as it was. The charge was higher than
at the Dame Schools, from 6d. to 9d. a week, and the
average master made 16s. or 17s. a week, the capable
master a good deal more. Too often the teacher's qualification for his job was that noted in the case of the
old men who kept Dame Schools: " unfitness for every
other." These masters and mistresses, however, had a
better opinion of themselves than that held by their
investigators. " Some intelligent masters," it was said,
" . . . conceive there is something in the occupation
which begets self-sufficiency." Whatever the truth of this,
these Common Day School masters were " strongly im-
pressed with the superiority of their own plans to those
of any other school, and very little inclined to listen to
any suggestions respecting improvements in the system
of education that had been made in other places." These
schools professed to teach reading, writing, and arithmetic. Penmanship was considered essential, and specimens of fine writing were exhibited to attract parents. In
some of the better ones a little grammar and geography
were thrown in for an extra penny or so a week. Occasionally they soared higher. In one school the master

dilated on the various sciences he could teach: Hydraulics, Hydrostatics, Geography, Geology, Etymology, Entomology. The visitor remarked: "This is *multum in parvo* indeed." To which the master immediately replied: "Yes, I teach that: you may put that down too."

The premises of these schools were not much better than those of the Dame Schools. Perhaps the worst example was a school in Liverpool, where a garret, measuring 10 feet by 9 feet, contained one master, one cock, two hens, three black terriers, and forty children. Bad air, dirty rooms, incompetent teachers, disorderly ways ("tiresome task this teaching," remarked one master, "there is no managing them"), absence of books or other apparatus, were characteristics of these schools. A floating population of boys and girls resorted to them; in most boys' schools there were some girls, and in most girls' schools some boys, and the children learnt or failed to learn the elements of the three R's, to the constant accompaniment of the birch. On the other hand, the masters and mistresses were occasionally persons of ability, and even when ability was absent there was also an absence of the monotony and routine which improved methods often brought with them. School life must have had attractions and surprises under the master who was met by the investigator "issuing from his school at the head of all his scholars, to see a fight in the neighbourhood; and instead of stopping to reply to any educational queries, only uttered a breathless invitation to come along and see the sport." These schools were severely blamed for their neglect of any systematic religious and moral instruction, but a good many children surfeited with this teaching in National or Lancastrian schools might have done better in the care of the master who, when asked his method of religious teaching,

answered " I hear them their catechism once a week," and
to the question how he taught morals, replied, " I tell
them to be good lads, you know, and mind what I say to
them, and so on." Perhaps they might have done no
worse under the gentleman who, when asked if he taught
morals, observed: " That question does not belong to my
school, it belongs to the girls' schools." One of these
masters, held up to ridicule in the Manchester Report,
seems to have been before his time. He stated that " he
had adopted a system which he thought would at once
supply the great desiderata in education. ' It is simply,'
he said, ' in watching the dispositions of the children and
putting them especially to that particular thing which
they take to.' In illustration of this system, he called
up a boy of about ten years of age, who had *taken to*
Hebrew, and was just beginning to learn it; the master
acknowledging that he himself was learning too, in order
to teach his pupil. On being asked whether he did not
now and then find a few who did not take to anything,
he acknowledged that it was so, and this, he said, was the
only weak point in his system, as he feared that he should
not be able to make much of those children."

It might have happened that the boy whose experiences
we are attempting to imagine, instead of going to one of
the ramshackle, self-supporting schools, went instead to
a school dependent on public subscription and conducted
on the lines of one of the two societies for educating the
poor, whose methods and rivalries fill so much of the
educational literature of the time. In the Manchester Lancasterian School, connected with the British and Foreign
School Society, he would have found over a thousand
close-packed children, sitting on benches, all being taught
together in one room, with only two masters and one
mistress in charge. At first the noise would have been

deafening, the crowd bewildering, but soon he would
have noticed that there was order and system in the
apparent chaos, that the multitude obeyed certain words
and commands such as " sling hats," " clean slates," and
acted as one child, that each nine or ten boys were in
charge of another boy called a monitor, who taught them
the lesson that he had lately learned himself, either
summoning them to stand round him in one of the semi-
circles marked in the passage at the end of the forms and
teaching them to read from a board with the lesson
printed large upon it, or else standing at the end of the
form on which they were sitting and dictating to them
words of the number of syllables suitable to their particular class. Dictation for the whole school was a triumph
of organization. On the platform at one end sat the
master, and at a signal from him, or from the " monitor-
general," a sort of sergeant-major amongst children, the
monitor of the highest class would lead off with his four-
syllabled word, followed in turn by each monitor in the
hierarchy down to the bottom. When the process had
been repeated for six words, each monitor examined the
slates of his charges and signalled to the master by means
of a " telegraph " or signboard fixed at the end of the
form; as soon as corrections were made, and all the
telegraphs turned the right way, the master gave the
signal again and another six words were dictated.

If the boy were specially bright he might find himself,
even at the early age of seven, chosen by the master to be
trained as a monitor. The master would teach him a
lesson and he would repeat it like a little gramophone
to his small group. His authority over his group or
" draft " would not extend to chastisement, but he was
expected to become a rather stern disciplinarian. If he
perceived " a pupil untidy, talking, or idle," it was " his

duty to put a disgrace or accusation-mark about his neck, having first warned him." He was to take away the disgrace-mark as soon as the pupil showed that he was corrected of his fault, or as soon as he perceived " that another pupil had committed a similar offence." " Incorrigible pupils " he would send up to the master's platform. Even these boys were not whipped, for in marked contrast to the Common Day Schools, the Lancasterian and National Schools trusted to a system of rewards and of confinement for their discipline. Dirty boys were " sentenced to have their faces and hands washed before the whole school and to be confined for half an hour "; talkers, players, and idlers were also given half an hour's confinement, but by an ingenious arrangement of barter each half-hour's confinement could be paid for by a " merit ticket." But those culprits whose supply of tickets failed were " taken to the bottom of the school by the monitor of bad boys," and there made to do dictation of an appropriate kind for the allotted period. Good boys and monitors could exchange their merit tickets, each of which was worth half a farthing, for books or clothing at the end of the month.

School began and ended with the reading by the master of a chapter of the Bible; the Bible was the only reading-book, and on the Bible all lessons were based. In some schools there were libraries from which the more promising pupils might borrow books to read out of school hours, but these books generally had " a bearing towards the works of God or the word of God." By 1831, in order to counteract the deadly effects of mechanical instruction which were very obvious, attempts were made to teach the children the meaning of the words or sentences that they read or spelt or wrote, by a system of interrogation that had been hitherto confined to the highest class. Thus if the reading lesson had consisted of the first verse of Genesis, the following interrogation would take place:

> " *Monitor.* Who created the heavens and the earth?
> *Pupil.* God.
> *Monitor.* When did God create the heavens and the earth?
> *Pupil.* In the beginning.
> *Monitor.* What did God do in the beginning?
> *Pupil.* He created the heavens and the earth," etc., etc.

If the boy remained long enough at school he would learn reading, writing, and the first four rules of arithmetic; if he stayed longer he would be instructed in " geography both ancient and modern." This, as we shall see, contained also scraps of historical information. We will take a sample lesson, which was the ideal for the most forward children. Tyre was the subject. The monitor had loaded his own mind with various particulars about Tyre, acquired either from the master or from books studied in the school library. He would then, supposing there was a map, put it up, point out the position of Tyre, and proceed to relate his various items of information. After this he would question them on what he had told them, as follows:

> " *Monitor.* Where is it?
> *Pupil.* On an Island.
> *Monitor.* Describe the situation of the Island?
> *Pupil.* It is at the eastern extremity of the Levant, opposite the northern part of the Holy Land, from which it is separated by a narrow strait.
> *Monitor.* What occasioned its erection on an Island?
> *Pupil.* Its being attacked by Nebuchadnezzar.
> *Monitor.* In what tribe was it included?

Pupil. Asshur.

Monitor. For what was it remarkable?

Pupil. Commercial prosperity.

Monitor. In what class of powers should we place it?

Pupil. Naval.

Monitor. Was the second Tyre ever taken?

Pupil. Yes.

Monitor. By whom?

Pupil. Alexander the Great.

Monitor. Cite a passage of Scripture relating to that event?

Pupil. Isaiah xxiii.

Monitor. What is Tyre now?

Pupil. A place resorted to by fishermen to dry their nets.

Monitor. The prophecy respecting this?

Pupil. Ezekiel xxvi. 14."

And so on, till Ezekiel, Isaiah, Alexander and Nebuchadnezzar were exhausted.

In the thirties, and still more in the forties, an attempt was made to relax the strict reference of all knowledge in the Lancasterian Schools to the Scriptures, and though no language was taught, ample explanations were given of the roots of words. This was probably not unconnected with the fact noticed by Kay-Shuttleworth: " Those who have had close intercourse with the labouring classes well know with what difficulty they comprehend words not of a Saxon origin, and how frequently addresses to them are unintelligible from the continual use of terms of a Latin or Greek derivation. . . ." A short illustration will show how it was attempted to make these words intelligible. In the highest divisions of the school, reading-books containing varied subjects, including "general history, physics, and natural history," had been introduced. A lesson on natural history would be given thus. The boys would read: " Ruminating animals. Cud-chewing or ruminating animals form the *eighth* order. These, with the exception of the camel, have no cutting teeth in the upper jaw, but their place is supplied with a hard pad. In the lower jaw there are eight cutters; the tearers, in general, are absent, so that there is a vacant space between the cutters and grinders. The latter are very broad, and are kept rough and fit for grinding the vegetable food on which these animals live, by the enamel being disposed in crescent-shaped ridges." And so on for a long time. Interrogation on this lesson would then take place:

Monitor. What have you been reading about?
Boy. Ruminating animals.
Monitor. Another name for ruminating?
Boy. Cud-chewing.
Monitor. What is the root of the word?
Boy. ' Rumen,' the cud.
Monitor. What does the termination *ate* mean?
Boy. To do or act on in some way.
Monitor. Ruminate, then, is to——?
Boy. To act on the cud,"

and so on. And later:

"*Monitor.* You read in the lesson *the enamel is disposed in crescent-shaped ridges.* What is the enamel?
Boy. The hard, shining part of the tooth.
Monitor. What part of our tooth is it?
Boy. The covering of that part that is out of the jaw-bone.
Monitor. What do you mean by disposed?

Boy. Placed.
Monitor. The root?
Boy. ' Pono,' I place.
Monitor. What is crescent-shaped?
Boy. Shaped like the moon before it is a half-moon.
Monitor. Draw a crescent. (*Boys draw it on the black-board.*)
Monitor. What is the root of the word?
Boy. ' Cresco,' I grow," etc., etc., etc.

It is not remarkable to read in a footnote, " At this point it would be necessary for the monitor to put many of these questions over again, to ascertain that there has been perfect comprehension of the subject."

Possibly during his school years the boy's parents would move house, and it would be more convenient to send him to a school under the auspices of the National Society for Promoting the Education of the Poor in the Principles of the Established Church. He would prob-ably have noticed little difference. The forms would be arranged differently, but he would still be taught by monitors or teach others as a monitor. The repertory of religious instruction would be enlarged; he would hear a good deal about something called doctrines; in place of continual " catechetical interrogation " on the text of the Bible, he would now learn to repeat the creeds and the catechism, whilst words like " justification " and " sanctification " would loom large on his horizon. If he stayed long enough at school, he might know less about the connection of Tyre with Nebuchadnezzar and Alex-ander than if he had stopped at the Lancasterian School, but on the other hand he might hope to rival the class of children, aged ten to fourteen, described by Bishop Blomfield, who passed an excellent examination in the first nine chapters of Romans, explaining any passage on which they were questioned, and referring readily to parallel passages, and this in addition to showing knowledge of " almost all the principal facts connected with the history of the New Testament, the application of the leading prophecies, and the common geography of the Holy Land."

On leaving school the boy we have tried to describe might not be altogether clear in his head about the doctrine of redemption and sanctification, or the pomps and vanities of the world, but he would have been still more puzzled to explain the declaration of the National Society whose school he had been attending, that they would not " timorously, unwisely and supinely . . . give up into the Hands of our Enemies that sacred and victorious weapon, which we have so long and successfully wielded in the Defence and Preservation of the Religion, the Virtue, the Welfare and Happiness of our Country." To understand it he would have had to know something of the history of education during the preceding thirty years. That history would have made him aware that all the while, over the unsuspecting heads of the little boys and girls in the " Society " schools who were busy spelling out " The way of God is a good way," or " Bad men are foes to God," or adding up the children produced by Jacob's various wives, a battle was raging among the Olympians for the possession of their young souls. A brief sketch of that battle is essential if we are to understand the state of education when public help was first given to it.

At the end of the eighteenth and beginning of the nineteenth centuries, in the age of mechanical inventions, two remarkable men, Dr. Andrew Bell, a Church of England clergyman, and Joseph Lancaster, a Quaker, invented separately new and similar systems of teaching. Both discovered that education could be greatly cheapened by the employment of child labour; schoolmasters, except as heads, were superfluous; scholars could be used to teach each other. For the credit of this discovery there was fierce controversy between the partisans of the two men. Lancaster began his teaching career in London: Bell started his system as a chaplain in Madras, and hence it was often called the "Madras system." Never have educationalists or their friends made higher claims. Lancaster, who announced that he had "invented, under the blessing of Divine Providence, a new and mechanical system of Education," showed that one master "might conduct a school of 1,000 children with perfect ease." Bell, who had a lively fancy, though he did not mention the figure of a thousand, was no less sanguine. "On this principle a superior can conduct any institution, how numerous soever, through the instrumentality of its own members. In a school it gives to the master the hundred eyes of Argus, the hundred hands of Briareus, and the wings of Mercury. In other words, by multiplying his ministers at pleasure it gives to him indefinite powers, and enables him to instruct as many pupils as any school will contain. While it bears a manifest analogy to the mechanical powers, it infinitely surpasses them in simplicity, economy, force, and effect. With great propriety it has been called the STEAM ENGINE of the MORAL WORLD. The intellectual machinery costs nothing, grows in force and efficiency, by the use that is made of it, and with the work which it has to perform: viresque acquirit eundo. In a word, it is the *lever of Archimedes* transferred from matter to mind." Nor were his adherents less enthusiastic in their language. "If we do not reproach the philosophers of old time with the ignorance of what a Newton saw and investigated, we must not find fault with those good men for not having forestalled the merits and anticipated the discoveries of a Bell," said the Dean of Chichester of those who had tried to educate the young in the past. The new arrangement of the school-room seemed indeed to make it possible to educate a large number of children at a small expense. "Suppose," wrote Bell, "that in two empires consisting each of 2,000,000 children to be educated, the one on the old plan, in schools of 50 pupils each, the other on the new, of 500, at the stipend of £50 to each master. The amount of school fees, in the one case, would be £1 a scholar, or £2,000,000; in the other, 2s. a scholar, or £200,000—the difference being £1,800,000. But, allowing the Madras master double this stipend, the difference would then be £1,600,000."

Enthusiasts for education grouped themselves behind the two men according to their colour, and societies were founded to promote their respective principles. The Lancasterian Society (1808), afterwards called the British and Foreign School Society (1814), was unsectarian, and drew its main support from Whigs and Nonconformists. In its schools the Bible was taught without comment. The Society which followed Dr. Bell was called "The National Society for Promoting the Education of the Poor in the Principles of the Established Church," and taught Church doctrines as well as the Scriptures. The National Society, in addition to its enthusiasts, harnessed to its purposes a good many who had before been lukewarm, if not hostile, to scattering schooling wholesale. William Cotton, the philanthropist, giving evidence on behalf of the National Society, summed the matter up very justly, when he said that whilst the main supporters and real workers (of the National Society) were quite unaffected by any question of rivalry, yet " the success of Joseph Lancaster created a considerable sensation among those who were not very friendly to the education of the poor, but who would rather see the people educated by the National Church than by Joseph Lancaster, I readily admit." However this may be, and whatever the motives of its subscribers, the National Society was the wealthier of the two.

Let us now consider the position of education for the working classes when the Reformed Parliament began to sit in 1833. Whitbread in 1807, and after him Brougham, had pressed in vain for some scheme of national education. A large number of the existing schools were still (specially in towns) affairs of private enterprise. The extent to which the working classes in the industrial towns were supporting schools out of their pockets has perhaps been overlooked. In Manchester, for 4,070 children attending schools that were either free or partially assisted, there were 13,108 children attending entirely self-supporting schools. In Bury, the proportions were 652 to 1,799. In Salford, 1,950 to 3,709. In Birmingham, 4,066 to 8,248. In West Bromwich, 423 to 1,131. In York, where there were many endowments, the figures were reversed, for there were 2,697 free and assisted scholars to 1,294 in self-supporting schools. In Bristol and Liverpool, too, there was a small majority of free and assisted scholars. In Bristol, the figures were 7,207 to 6,494; in Liverpool, 13,000 to 12,000. If the facts elicited by the Manchester Statistical Society about Rutland may be taken as typical, there was a majority in country districts of free and assisted scholars; in Rutland the figures were 1,610 to 1,218. The payments at the self-supporting schools in all the places investigated were much the same; 3d. to 4d. was usual at Dame Schools, 8d. to

9d. at the Common Day Schools. The Bristol Statistical Society made the interesting calculation that in that town, out of a population of some 120,000, working-class parents were paying no less than £15,202 19s. 6d. for the education of their children, that is, more than half the total parliamentary grant.

Important though these self-supporting schools were, public interest was centred on the work and the rivalries of the two Societies. That there was a lamentable deficiency in means of education was generally agreed; the full extent of that deficiency was a matter of guesswork. An ambitious attempt to clear the ground before action was made early in the new Parliament by Lord Kerry, who asked (May 24, 1833) for a return, which amounted to an educational census. Rickman, who had achieved brilliant results with the population returns, took it in hand, unpaid. The answers to the 15,000 circulars, enclosing elaborate schedules, sent out to overseers, were remarkably numerous and full. From this portentous mass of information, published in three volumes, it was calculated that out of an estimated population for England and Wales of 14,400,000, 1,276,947 children, or 1 in 11 of the population, were attending day schools of some sort or other, whilst 1,548,890, or 1 in 9 of the population, were attending Sunday-schools. Unfortunately, although the returns were numerous and full, they were found on more careful investigation to be hopelessly incorrect. As an example, the Manchester Statistical Society found that in Manchester, where the total school-going population was about 18,500, allowing for certain mistakes which cancelled each other, the Kerry returns omitted 181 schools with 8,646 scholars. The truth was that the attempt was too ambitious. The experiences of the Manchester investigator throw light on the errors.

At York, the masters of the Endowed and Charity Schools
" answered all interrogations with the utmost caution
and in the vaguest manner," each seeming to think that
his own school could be omitted without affecting the
accuracy of the total.   At Salford, many of the mistresses,
with a caution for which one cannot blame them, asked
a " prudent neighbour " to come in before answering the
questions. If *viva voce* questions were bad, elaborate
schedules were worse.   Apart from the universal dislike
of filling up forms, detailed knowledge of the Scriptures
had persuaded some that counting numbers was unlucky.
" No, no," said one teacher, " you shan't catch me counting; see what a pretty mess David made of it when he
counted the children of Israel."

Whilst the Kerry papers were being sent out the
Government took two important steps.   In the first place,
they included in their Factory Act of 1833 provisions for
the compulsory education of factory children.   On paper
every child was obliged to attend school for two hours a
day, and if a suitable school was wanting, the Inspector
was " authorized to establish or procure the establishment of such schools."   As, however, no funds were
provided, and as the relevant sections were carelessly
drafted, these well-intentioned provisions were often a
dead-letter, and, where carried out conscientiously by
employers, were a tax on industry.   The second step
taken by the Government was to make a grant in aid of
education.   Their plan avoided the pitfalls of religious
controversy.   They gave £20,000 to be divided between
the two Societies, in aid of subscriptions for building
schools.

In the course of the next five years a good deal of light
was thrown on the state of popular education in the
reports of three Parliamentary Committees.   The evidence

given before these committees showed clearly that the most serious evil was the lack of effective provision for training teachers. The National Society took young men and women at the age of twenty-one onwards and gave them five months' training. Most of them had tried other professions or callings; some had come from " very respectable situations in life in which they have not been successful." The British and Foreign Society took them from nineteen years old to twenty-three or twenty-four. Their candidates were mostly ex-mechanics who had acquired a taste for teaching by helping in Sunday-schools. If they kept any of that taste after the three months' intensive training that was given them, they must have been remarkable persons. " Our object," said the Secretary, " is to keep them incessantly employed from five in the morning until nine or ten at night. We have rather exceeded in the time devoted to study the limit we would choose, on account of the very short period we are able to keep them, and we have found in some instances that their health has suffered on account of their having been previously quite unaccustomed to mental occupations." The future schoolmistresses seem to have stood the training even less successfully.

In 1839 Lord John Russell made a serious effort to meet this need. He set up a Committee of the Privy Council, consisting of four Cabinet Ministers with a Secretary and two Inspectors, who were to disseminate a knowledge of improvements among those engaged in education and to keep the Committee informed of progress. Dr. Kay, afterwards better known as Sir James Kay-Shuttleworth, was the first Secretary. He was a great public servant of independent mind and enlightened ideas, of whom Sir Michael Sadler has said: " To him more than to anyone else we owe it that England is supplied with schools for the children of her people, and that this costly work has been accomplished without a breach between Church and State."

Part of the Government scheme was the establishment of a Government Normal School for training teachers, and a Model School in connection with it. This proposal caused a storm. The Church was outraged because in the Model School, attached to the Normal School, religious instruction was divided into "general" and "special," and the special instruction might be given, if desired, by Dissenting ministers. The candidate teachers in the Normal School could also have their special religious instruction provided from Nonconformist sources. This was taken to foreshadow a general "right of entry" into all schools. Nor were certain Nonconformists any better pleased. In the regulation that "either at the time fixed for reading the Scriptures, or at the hours of special instruction," Roman Catholics might read their own version of the Bible, the Wesleyan Methodists saw the triumph of the Scarlet Woman. This recognition by the State of "the corrupted Romish translations" they declared to be "a direct violation of the first principles of our Protestant Constitution."

The Government, to use Lord John Russell's expression, threw the Normal School to the wolves. The wolves tore the corpse and called for fresh victims. In a vigorous debate on the order for a Committee of Supply on June 14, adjourned till June 19 and 20, Lord Stanley, declaring that "education was the peculiar province of the clergy and was a spiritual matter to be entrusted to their superintendence," demanded the rescinding of the Order of the Council. Statistics, always a special feature of debates on education, were hurled backwards and forwards with equal effect to prove opposite conclusions.

Prisons and penitentiaries were ransacked to show that education cured or encouraged crime. In the end the Government only escaped defeat by five votes (280 to 275). Four days later, when Lord John Russell moved the vote of £30,000 for education, the majority was still narrower, 275 to 273. In the Commons the Government had scraped through and had saved the grant by two votes; in the Lords, faced with episcopal rhetoric, they could not avoid censure. The Archbishop of Canterbury (July 5) proposed and carried a series of resolutions drawn up by Peel deprecating the Government's action, and proposing to present an address to Her Majesty to ask that no plan for general education should be established without consulting the House of Lords.

In 1839 the Whig Government had only saved itself by throwing important limbs to the wolves of the Church; in 1843 when the next attempt was made to improve education, this time by a Conservative Government, the wolves of Dissent claimed and obtained the whole corpse. Yet the proposals were made in one respect under favourable conditions. The riots of 1842 had caused general alarm, and Ashley, taking advantage of this mood, had carried a resolution in the House of Commons on the need for popular education. Sir James Graham in reply lamented that England had failed to profit by the warning of the French Revolution which might have taught the sects to moderate their quarrels. His new proposals were part of a Factory Bill, and meant in the first instance for factory children, but he hoped that the new schools would provide education for all children in factory districts. But his schools never came to life. The Nonconformists raised a storm, objecting partly because they thought the Church was given too much power in the management of the schools, and partly because the Sunday-

schools might suffer. Graham went far to meet these
objections, but the Nonconformists did not relax their
hostility and he had to drop the scheme. He could have
carried it through Parliament, but he might have been
met by passive resistance when the schools were set up.
Brougham described the position: "The Church was
anxious to educate the people, but the Church was still
more anxious to get the better of the sects; the sects were
anxious to have popular education, but the sects were
still more anxious than this to overturn the Church."

In July 1846 the Whigs again came into power, and
the insistent Kay-Shuttleworth pressed his reforms with
fresh ardour. Statistics about illiteracy were beginning
to alarm politicians. Each year since 1839 the Registrar-
General had given the number of married persons who
signed with a mark. This percentage had remained
practically unchanged. It had been 41·6 in 1839 (men,
33·7; women, 49·5), it remained at from 40 to 41·4 during
the next six years. Yet schools had undoubtedly increased
during the school years of the brides and bridegrooms.
No time was lost. In August an outline of the new
proposals was issued, followed in December by further
details. The proposals consisted of an elaborate scheme
for the reorganization of school teaching, and the improvement of the teachers' position. Monitors were to
be replaced wherever possible by pupil teachers, appren-
ticed for five years. Grants were to be given to the pupil
teachers and to the teachers who trained them. When
the apprenticeship was finished, the further training of
the pupil teachers for three years at a normal school was
to be encouraged by a system of scholarships and grants.
Teachers thus trained were to enjoy certain additions
to their salaries provided by grants, and retiring pensions
were to be given under certain conditions. The estab-

lishment of the pupil teacher system in a school, and the additions to salaries, were dependent on a favourable report from an inspector, and it was an inspector who conducted each year the examination of the pupil teachers. Thus the Education Committee for the first time obtained a certain control over the schools it inspected and subsidized. The qualifications of the pupil teachers for giving religious instruction were to be tested in Church Schools by the inspector, with the assistance of the parochial clergyman; in other schools the managers were merely required to certify that they were satisfied with the candidates' religious knowledge.

These proposals were not an attempt to grasp English education and remould it into a national scheme. No Government was likely to try its hand at that for some time. They were a scheme for improving existing schools without altering the existing basis.

The Nonconformists again attacked the scheme, this time with the support of Bright, who had just entered Parliament and tried to answer Macaulay's argument that it was the duty of the State to educate the people. Fortunately Bright's view, that it was better to leave the nation to such arrangements as we have described rather than run the risk of increasing the influence of the Church, was so completely discredited by the facts that had been made public that the Government had no difficulty in holding to their plan, though Macaulay lost his seat in consequence.

Most of our knowledge about schools in the forties comes from inspectors' reports, and these, of course, deal mainly with the grant-aided Church or Society Schools. Now it would be possible to pick out things said of these schools by the inspectors as harsh as anything said of the Common " Adventure " Schools by the Manchester

Statistical Society, but we must not assume that they were worse than they had been; probably they were a good deal better. The truth was that the inspectors were the first people who discovered that a fog enveloped the children's minds, and that it was possible to read intelligently and even to answer questions correctly without having the slightest notion of the meaning of the words uttered. Any deviation from routine produced chaos. Mr. Tremenheere, examining the British Schools, put his questions in unexpected order:

" *Q*. Who were the Gentiles?—*A*. People of God.

Q. Who was Moses?—*A*. Apostle of Christ.

Q. Who was Peter?—*A*. An angel.

Q. Where was Christ crucified?—*A*. England.

Q. Who was Jesus Christ the son of?—*A*. Son of David.

Q. Who then was David?—*A*. Son of Jesus."

The National Schools with their catechism provided equally striking examples.

" *Q*. Who gave you the name which you received in baptism?—*A*. God.

Q. What did your godfathers and godmothers promise and vow for you respecting the pomps and vanities of the world?—*A*. All the sinful lusts of the flesh.

Q. I asked what they promised and vowed respecting the pomps of the world?—*A*. That I should believe all the articles of the Christian faith.

Q. What do you mean by those articles?—(Silence.) The articles of the faith means all the truths of the gospel; will you tell me any one of the truths of the gospel which your godfathers vowed you should believe?

—Five were silent, the sixth answered, 'The Command-
ments.'"

But though the children might seem to have lapsed
into what Mr. Moseley, the inspector with perhaps the
most vivid pen, called "that vagrant state of mind,
approaching to idiocy," yet, if appropriately handled,
they could perform feats at the public examinations held
before admiring subscribers, causing the audience, in the
same inspector's bitter words, to "go away with the
impression that the children of the poor are receiving a
better education than they did themselves." The feats
of etymology or mental arithmetic were "wonderful only
as long as the short methods used in producing them are
unknown." Etymology itself he described as a method
of "directing their attention to the derivation of one
language, with which they are comparatively unacquainted, from another, of which they are profoundly
ignorant."

The severest indictment of the elementary education of
this time was made, not by the school inspectors, but by
the Children's Employment Commission in their Second
Report of 1843 (p. 202). "In all the districts," they
stated, "many Children who had been returned as able
to read, when examined were found to know only the
letters of the alphabet; a very small proportion indeed
being able to read well an easy book. Even of those
who could read fluently, very few, when questioned,
were found to have any conception of the meaning of the
words they uttered, or were able to give any intelligible
account of what seemed to the examiners to be simple
and easy terms and things; so that, as far as regards the
acquisition of any useful knowledge, or the accomplish-
ment of any higher purpose to be answered by education,

these Children, in great numbers of instances, were as little benefited, after years of so-called tuition, as if they had never been at any school." Mr. Moseley in 1845 calculated that out of the 11,782 children covered by his inspection, some 75 per cent. would leave school unable " to read the Scriptures with tolerable ease or correctness." Mr. Watkins reported in 1846 that out of 15,466 children in the schools he visited, a little under half were in the elementary stages of learning to read, whilst about a quarter could read simple narratives, and a quarter could read with ease. When we remember the short time spent at school it seems remarkable that the percentage of illiteracy was so low.

From one aspect it is fortunate that these schools housed a fleeting population. Lyon Playfair, writing of the Lancashire schools, says in the Health of Towns Commission Report, " It is by no means an uncommon thing, on entering public schools, to observe children carried out in a fainting state, and the visitor, who feels the contaminated state of the air on entering it from a purer atmosphere, cannot be astonished at the occurrence."

This detailed examination of the state of the schools brings out the importance of the Minutes of 1846. The pupil teacher system has an ugly sound in the ears of a generation unacquainted with monitors. The reforms of 1846 recognized, however imperfect their plan, and methods, that the great discovery for which Bell and Lancaster disputed the credit, the discovery that children could be taught cheaply, had been a curse to education. The Government now set themselves with slow and feeble steps to the task of training efficient teachers, and creating efficient schools.

Though the education of children excited so absorbing a controversy, the education of adults was not altogether neglected. In practically every town of any size an intelligent workman who wanted to improve and educate himself would find by the forties a Mechanics' Institution, or some similar society. In England, in 1850, it was estimated that there were seven hundred of these societies with 107,000 members. The libraries connected with them contained over 690,000 books. But though the figures sound impressive, these institutions caused much searching of heart. They had failed to fulfil the expectations of their founders. Their rate of mortality was high, though their birth-rate was also high, and even in those that were comfortably established the membership was apt to fluctuate with alarming rapidity. To understand their position, it is necessary to glance back at their origins.

These institutions were started by Brougham and Birkbeck at a time when, as a writer described it, " there still prevailed in many quarters a strong jealousy of any political discussion by the people, and still more of any society which proposed to assemble periodically several hundreds of the labouring classes. Hence their founders, in their desire to conciliate opposition, banned political or religious discussion or books, and forbade newspapers. Even so, the *St. James' Chronicle* could say of the London Mechanics' Institution in 1825, " A scheme more completely adapted for the destruction of this empire could not have been invented by the author of evil himself than that which the depraved ambition of some men, the vanity of others, and the supineness of a third and more important class, has so nearly perfected." Even their advocates felt a certain need for apology: " I am at a loss," said Sir Benjamin Heywood, President of the Manchester Mechanics' Institution, in 1827, " to see how we are disturbing the proper station of the working classes, and giving them an undue elevation; we do not alter their relative position; a spirit of intellectual activity, unequalled in any age or country, now prevails amongst us, and, if the superstructure be renewed and strengthened, it does not seem fitting that the foundation should be neglected."

Mechanics' Institutions were established in the hope of popularizing scientific knowledge, and incidentally making the workman better at his work. The latter motive at first received the chief emphasis. At Manchester, for example, the preamble declared that " This society was formed for the purpose of enabling Mechanics and Artizans of whatever trade they may be, to become acquainted with such branches of science as are of practical application in the exercise of that trade, that they may possess a more thorough knowledge of their business, acquire a greater degree of skill in the practice of it, and be qualified to make improvements and even new inventions in the Arts which they respectively profess." It was a time when there seemed no limit to the possibilities of scientific and mechanical discoveries, and it was hoped that the new institutions might benefit not only their members but science itself by " uniting and concentrating the scattered rays of genius, which might otherwise be dissipated and lost to the scientific world."

Mechanics' Institutions had the difficult task of providing instruction for students on very different levels of book learning. Many members could not even read or write. Hence the Institutions had not only to spread scientific truth, but to act as glorified evening elementary schools as well, with classes for reading, writing, and arithmetic. They provided courses of lectures, classes of various kinds, and libraries, with reading-rooms often attached to them. But when the first excitement and enthusiasm had worn off, numbers dwindled in an alarming manner. The cult of the lecture soon languished. " After the first novelty of listening to lectures is over, the workmen can rarely be induced to attend them," wrote a disillusioned observer in 1839. It was discovered that the topic of the steam engine roused no enthusiasm in manufacturing districts. " The jaded artisan," explained John Cleave in 1842, " needs some relaxation after the severe privations and enervating toils of the day, and however much he may desire scientific lore, will turn with disgust from the necessary instruction, if presented in a mere dry and detailed form, ungarnished by a palatable admixture of the lighter mental food of general literature." A correspondent of the *Poor Man's Guardian* put it more bluntly: " Many of us are already saturated with as much of what is called science as we can carry."

The art of popular lecturing was in its infancy, and, as a successful lecturer on non-scientific subjects to Mechanics' Institutions expressed it in 1849, " A man must have a very happy talent for lecturing if he succeeds in making scientific lectures popular." Let us imagine a workman, eager to know the secrets of the new balloons, attending Mr. Tatum's first lecture on *Aerostation* at the London Mechanics' Institution. This is what he would be told at the outset. " Before the principles of *Aerostation* could be properly comprehended, a knowledge of *Pneumatics* was requisite; and he had a right to presume, from the lectures which had been delivered on that subject, that the Members were acquainted with the nature and properties of *air*. A knowledge of *hydrostatics* is also essential to the study of a science which treats of bodies floating in a certain medium, by displacing a quantity of the fluid in which they float, equal in weight to the floating body. Besides this, it is necessary to know that *air* is a *gravitating medium*, and, therefore, not only *Pneumatics*, but *Hydrostatics* must be understood; so far, at least, as relates to the *specific gravities* of bodies. Chemistry also is necessary. . . ." It is not surprising that the workman was shy of the lecture-room, and that when he went there he preferred the lectures given by local men in language which he could understand.

In the places where numbers kept up, it was noticed that the members were no longer, as at first was the case, predominantly workmen; clerks and small craftsmen took their place. Enthusiasts could account for this by explaining that, thanks to the opportunities for improvement, members rose in the social scale, and the institution rose with them, but this was not the usual view. Hudson has an interesting description of the way in which middle-aged professional men, and heads of firms, invaded the Athenæums, ousting the young clerks for whom they were intended. The clerks, in their turn, anxious to avoid the society of " the governor," joined the Mechanics' Institutions, where " the warehouseman, the packer, the carter, and the mill-hand shun the society of the clerk and the foreman, and . . . in turn quit the Institution which was established expressly for them."

Attempts were made to improve the libraries at Mechanics' Institutions. These libraries, whose totals of books often sounded very imposing, suffered from being composed largely of gifts. A lecturer who had made a special study of the subject described them vividly: " Many of the books are gift books, turned out of people's shelves, and are never used, and old magazines of different kinds, so that, out of 1,000 volumes, perhaps there may be only 400 or 500 useful ones. The rest are, many of them, only annual registers and old religious magazines, that are never taken down from the shelves." Samuel Smiles,

who was well acquainted with the Yorkshire Institutions,
said much the same thing: "Many of the books in Mechanics' Institutions are very unattractive; many of those
books, for instance, which are given by way of presents,
are books which nobody would think of reading nowa-
days; a large proportion of them are dull, heavy books."
He remarked truly that to make a library successful there
must be money for buying fresh books. Fiction was
now made an important feature of the libraries, and it
was even complained of the various Manchester Mechanics' Institutions in 1849 that they were "in the hands
of a party who buy amusing books, and those who are
really disposed to improve themselves have no voice."

Mechanics' Institutions, then, useful though they were,
failed to accomplish all that was expected of them. Their
founders had overestimated the zeal for knowledge in the
working classes. They pictured all workmen, or at any
rate all skilled workmen, as craving for instruction, like
the Birmingham men of whom a successful lecturer at
Mechanics' Institutions spoke in 1849. "I have known
men rise at five and work till eight for book money, and
then go to their day's work." He could pick out, he said,
five or six working men as amongst the most intelligent
and best-read persons in Birmingham. "They are men
who have wrestled it out." But the cold fact is that the
passion for knowledge is not widely distributed in any
class, and when sacrifices must be made to satisfy it, the
distribution is narrower still. Before the Ten Hours Act,
too, many factory workers must have been physically
debarred from attending lectures or classes. That, con-
sidering the circumstances, a remarkable desire for knowledge existed, was shown not only in the attendance, such
as it was, at the Mechanics' Institutions, but in the
numbers of small so-called Mutual Improvement Societies

that sprang up, some of them mushroom growths that soon died away, others developing into organized societies. A few working men would meet regularly in the evenings " to improve themselves by mutual intercourse," and this sometimes led to the starting of regular classes. The Leeds Mutual Improvement Society, started by four young men in 1844, went through a stage when "reading, writing, grammar, and arithmetic, were taught and learned amidst rakes, and hoes, and broken flowerpots" in an old garden house. By 1850 it was giving classes on subjects including Discussion, Chemistry, and French to eighty members, in extensive premises in a back yard off Kirkgate. There was a special crop of these informal and unpretentious gatherings in the northern counties in 1849 and 1850, largely, no doubt, as the result of the Ten Hours Act. Even lectures of the right kind, given by the right kind of man, could be a success, as was shown by the case of Mr. Richardson, a self-educated teacher, who for fifteen years, in 1850, had gone round as a peripatetic lecturer on Science to the scattered northern villages, where " the toiling mining population of Durham and Northumberland proceed over the hills in rain, sleet, and frost, that they may learn the great truths which civilization has made manifest." He lectured on Electricity, Pneumatics, etc., " travelling day by day, by cart, by rail and by coach far from the great towns and public highways, with his extensive and beautiful electrical apparatus, valued at £500." " Somewhat provincial in his dialect, perfect as a manipulator, and correct in his statements, he never fails to interest and instruct."

The original hope that Mechanics' Institutions, once established with help from benevolent persons, would become self-supporting, soon vanished. The system of quarterly subscriptions, even when fixed at the low rate of three shillings, as at Birmingham, was unpopular with workmen. If the sum was raised the numbers fell off. There were no endowments from pious founders and benefactors; living benefactors were essential and were often generous, but in addition there was a constant campaign to raise funds by means of bazaars, exhibitions, and soirées. Though the museums of stuffed natural-history specimens or models of machinery usually became neglected dust traps, instead of producing the intellectual elevation expected from them, a great appetite existed for temporary exhibitions. At Liverpool three exhibitions between 1840 and 1844 raised £5,000 for the Mechanics' Institution. Patent ice, cartoons, dissolving views, a panorama, evening concerts, and a diving-bell were among the attractions. It is clear that much of the energy that should have been spent on spreading educa-tion was devoted to these campaigns for raising funds.

It was complained that whilst working-class energy was spent liberally on efforts to make a success of " provident societies, trade societies, temperance societies, and the various political clubs that from time to time agitate the country, there is no evidence to show any of this spirit of proselytism in favour of Mechanics' Institutions." John Cleave answered that ill success was attributable, " not to the apathy of Working Men—but to their utter and just repugnance to institutions supported in a great measure by patronage and conducted by patronage." When we read in Hudson that " The lawned Divine, and the ermined Duke feel a pleasure in presiding over the festivals of the artizan and the day labourer," it is easy to understand that many artisans and day labourers preferred the small informal societies which they had created themselves, where the improvement was done by themselves and not by their betters. But when these small societies grew to any size, problems of finance became as acute as in the case of Mechanics' Institutions, and even Lovett's National Hall depended on " donations from benevolent individuals." Much gratuitous work was done, but premises had to be rented or maintained, teachers and lecturers of advanced subjects had to be paid, and the fees that could be charged without discouraging membership seldom covered the cost. How narrow was the margin even where the membership was satisfactory and enthusiastic was shown by the position of the Ancoats Lyceum in its flourishing days in 1841, when the income had exceeded the expenditure, but the Directors were warned that should they " take an injudicious step, such as engaging a Lecturer who should prove a failure, for three nights, at two guineas per night, this, with the expense of printing, would exhaust the surplus, and leave no attractions for the remainder of the quarter. . . ."

In 1841 (March 11) it was proposed in the House of Commons by Mr. Gillon that grants should be given to Mechanics' Institutions. He pointed out that Oxford and Cambridge received public money, and claimed the same privilege for advanced education for working men. Peel, then in opposition, blessed the project, but when he came into office he found the difficulties too formidable. The episode of the Hullah classes was a warning that any attempt to help adult education would involve the Government that made it in all the quarrels that had raged so fiercely over the education of children.

Hullah was a musician with a genius for teaching music and inspiring others with his own enthusiasm, whose powers Dr. Kay determined to enlist for English education. Under the auspices of the Committee of Council for Education, though without any financial help from them, Hullah started a singing school for school-masters at Exeter Hall in 1841, employing an adaptation of M. Wilhem's methods which he had studied in France. The success was extraordinary; the classes were thrown open to the public, and in addition to schoolmasters and mistresses, Sunday-school teachers, mechanics, and shopkeepers trooped in. In 1842 over 3,000 persons were attending the classes held by Mr. Hullah and his assist-ants, and it was estimated that 50,000 school children in London were being taught on his method by teachers who had been trained in it. Unfortunately at the request of the pupils, three other classes were formed for teaching writing, arithmetic, and linear drawing, on the synthetic method. This proved fatal. When Parliament was asked for a grant for these classes the Bishop of London said that though he had been one of the original sub-scribers to the Hullah classes, this recent development had alarmed him. Classes were being established in different subjects without provision for religious instruc-tion. In this way you might even establish a normal school where no religion was taught. Peel was in favour of the grant and so were the Whigs, but he could not brave the frown of the Church, and reluctantly he put the plan on one side. Adult education had to wait for half a century for aid from Parliament.

E

CHAPTER VIII

REVOLT AND REFORM

THE significance of the revolt of the British people against the bleak conditions of its life, a revolt that began in 1830 and lasted nearly twenty years, has been obscured for some minds by its sober career. There were only two occasions in Chartist history when there was any serious attempt at violence. In November 1839 John Frost led a body of miners into Newport hoping to surprise the town and then to march to Monmouth to rescue Vincent, a Chartist orator, from prison. The miners were met by a small force of soldiers who killed or wounded a number of them and put the rest to immediate flight. In 1842 the Chartists took a leading part in conducting a series of strikes which had broken out in the North and the Midlands. They deprecated violence but urged the strikers to hold out until the Charter was conceded. The Government treated a manifesto which gave this advice as a treasonable document and sixty or seventy Chartists were transported by Special Commissions at Liverpool and Stafford.

The importance of the Chartist movement, like the importance of the great movement led by Owen that preceded it, consisted in the character of the discontent that produced it. In 1829 John Doherty created the

National Association for the Protection of Labour which soon collected 100,000 members. In 1833 Owen established the Grand National Consolidated Trades Union which embraced besides the great and powerful organizations, classes like agricultural labourers and women workers for whom combination seemed impossible except under some unusual stimulus of despair or excitement. The defeat of this movement was followed by Chartism, which, in its turn, collapsed in the spring of 1848.

All these movements had this in common, that they represented a revolt against a view of life. We give the name of Chartist to the London artisan who shared Lovett's enthusiasm for education and a cheap press; to the Birmingham politician who supported Attwood's campaign for a reform of the currency; to the Lancashire handloom weaver or the Yorkshire collier who listened to Oastler denouncing the new Poor Law, or Feargus O'Connor spinning project after project from his active and ill-ordered brain; to the South Wales miner who followed Frost with a pike to Newport and to prison. For though Chartism with its six points, adult suffrage, annual Parliaments, and the rest, had a definite programme, it was not a precise or logical demand for a particular reform; it was a protest as incoherent as the life that provoked it. Francis Place said on one occasion that the working man would not do anything even for his own advantage if that advantage be remote and that he had no desire to stir himself for the advantage of other persons. He hoped that education would produce a different temper. He referred to the education of the schools, but these men and women were learning in the school of life. For these movements show that men and women in their thousands were ready to follow any leader who promised them a radical change, whether he talked like Owen or Cobbett, like Oastler or O'Connor, whether he appealed to the ambitions of the trade unionist or the memories of the peasant, whether he offered to go forward or to go back, to build a golden future or recall a glittering past. For some ten years the English poor found in these agitations an opportunity of protesting against the place they occupied in the raw industrial settlements spreading over the Midlands and the North. This is the significance of the campaigns that began with Doherty's great combination and ended nearly twenty years later in the fiasco on Kennington Common.

That Chartism was not merely a political or merely an economic revolt is clear from the forms in which it found expression. Chartists protested, for example, against pew rents as a violation of the right of the people to their parish churches. Large numbers used to assemble before the hours of service, march to church, and occupy the seats. This was done in all the chief towns in 1839: in Manchester, Bradford, Newcastle, Bristol, Norwich, Bolton, Blackburn, Stockport, and other places. Disraeli said in *Sybil* that this plan very much affected "the imagination of the multitude." Sometimes the Chartists gave notice to the parson, and even suggested a text. Dr. Whittaker of Blackburn, having been invited to preach on the text, "Go to now, ye rich, weep and howl for your miseries that are coming upon you," explained that these words had no application to England "governed by equal laws." At Manchester the parson substituted his own text: "My house is a house of prayer, but you have made it a den of thieves." At Bury "the worthy Rector being fully prepared for their visit, gave them a lecture on keeping the peace and obeying the law which from its length as well as from its force, many of them would not exactly relish." In a few instances there was disorder. In most of the churches the Chartist congregations had to listen to critical sermons, but on one occasion they were specially invited to attend the Roman Catholic Cathedral at Norwich, where the preacher, taking as his text " Let him that hath two coats impart to him that hath none," preached an inflammatory sermon on the Reformation and the wrongs done by Protestants to the poor.

Not less significant was the establishment of Chartist Churches where the spirit and teaching of early Christianity attracted large numbers of men and women who found Church and Chapel alike cold and unsympathetic. The Report of the Midland Mining Commission described their widespread influence in some parts. One of their principal preachers, O'Neill, seems to have become as great a power among the Midland miners as Wesley himself had been a century earlier in Cornwall and Somerset. If the Chartists provided their own religion they provided also their own culture. In some towns under Owens' inspiration they founded Halls of Science. In Manchester a Hall of Science that cost £7,000 was built out of the savings of mechanics and artisans.

To regard Chartism as an episode, as an effort that failed, a flash in the pan, something to which you can give date of birth and death, is to misread the history of the time. The chief feature of that history is the growth and prevalence of discontent. No doubt that discontent was due to different causes and fed from different sources: the discomforts of the change from the life of the peasant or the artisan to that of the factory worker; the pressure from time to time of mass unemployment unrelieved by any remedy; the special hardships of the new Poor Law. But if its general character is to be described, it was discontent excited by the philosophy of life, of which the new town was the symbol and the expression. " The political economists in Church and State," said *The Crisis*, " are the real high priests of the realm. They have set up the golden calf. . . . Impious, dissatisfied people, say they, you men without property, mob and scum of the earth, with minds born to inferiority and hands made for our service. Why if you are still discontented do you not seek to accumulate wealth and so become respectable like ourselves? "

Joseph Toynbee tried to teach his generation that the " comforts of those who live by their labour did not by any means depend upon the mere money and amount of their wages." Chartism illustrated this truth. The discontent of which it was a symbol was provoked by an inequality that condemned the mass of the poor to a life without leisure or grace, without enjoyment or education, making them

> " A savage horde among the civilized,
> A servile band among the lordly free."

The workmen's newspapers and manifestoes show how conscious they were of the want of sympathy and colour in their surroundings; of the sharp division that was drawn between those who could enjoy life, and those who had to bear its burdens. For amid the triumphs of nature or of art, the masterpieces of God or man, there was nothing that seemed to belong to them, or to speak to them of a harmony that could subdue the spirit of strife and care. The *Pioneer*, a workman's paper, contrasted the bleak poverty of these towns with the full life of the ancient democracies, remarking that the oratorios in the Catholic churches had to satisfy and educate all the tastes and interests for which such lavish provision was made in Greece and Rome.

Chartism as a moral force was not extinguished by

defeat. Mill applied to its career the phrase, the victory
of the vanquished. The phrase was true in two senses.
Chartism went into different movements, like the movement for education, the movement for public health, the
trade union movement and the later franchise movement.
Long after the project of 1848 had collapsed amid the
relief and ridicule of London, Chartism was by these
means building up the self-respect of the English workman. But there is a second sense in which it was true.
For Lord John Russell admitted that it was the Chartist
movement that had turned the mind of the rulers of
England to these problems. Those rulers had forgotten
that if you want to satisfy a people, you must satisfy
instincts and tastes for which the new life for town and
industry made no provision. It is significant that the
Chartist agitation was followed by the Ten Hours Act of
1847, and the Public Health Act of 1848.

The most striking and important manifestation of the
new spirit was the success of the Ten Hours Bill. The Bill
won its way against the prestige and power of the ablest
and most experienced statesmen in public life. Peel, like
Cobden, believed that to pass the Ten Hours Bill was to
run the risk of industrial disaster. Nobody who heard
his speeches could think the danger illusory. He enjoyed
greater credit than any other man in public life. He had
been familiar from childhood with industrial problems;
he had extricated the finances of the nation from the
muddle left to him by his predecessors; he had taken part
in the reform of the factories; he had shown on the
income tax that he had larger views than the capitalists,
and on the Corn Laws that he had larger views than the
landlords; his skill and courage were unrivalled among
men who had taken part in government; of all debaters,
free alike from Bright's bitterness and Brougham's ped-

antry, he was the most persuasive, giving invariably the impression that he was anxious to answer a hard argument rather than to evade it. When he told his countrymen that the Ten Hours Bill was a public danger, no man of sense thought that he was saying what he did not believe, or that he believed what he was saying for frivolous reasons.

The House of Commons in 1847 decided to take the risk that Peel thought so menacing. And for what? To banish from English life a terrible formula, the phrase so long remembered in the mills of Lancashire, that the workman's life was eating, drinking, working, and sleeping. It was believed by the opponents of the Ten Hours Bill that this melancholy formula drove the wheels of Lancashire's industries and gave the English people their proud place in the world. The English people decided that they would risk the loss of that position rather than let that formula oppress their civilization any longer. It was a momentous choice, and the future of England turned on the answer. If this formula was to continue to rule her life the English town could not hope to escape from the gloom that darkened the thirties. "Schools and libraries are of small use without time to study," so ran the manifesto of the Short Time Central Committee in 1844. "Parks are well for those only who can have time to perambulate them, and baths are of little use to such dirty people as do not leave work till eight o'clock at night. We protest that it is a mere burlesque upon philanthropy to make provision for these benefits, with a continuance of twelve hours' labour and fifteen hours' occupation for every manufacturing operative above thirteen years of age." Every step taken towards civilizing town life meant only another contrast between rich and poor, if the workman was to be shut up in the mill, while

the well-to-do enjoyed themselves in the park and the
library. The Ten Hours Bill was in this sense the most
important event of the first half of the century. The
English people were trying to create a larger and more
generous life for the English town. The Ten Hours
Act meant that the workman was not to be shut out
of it.

Another proof of the change was the success of movements for supplying parks and playgrounds. In 1843
Birkenhead obtained a local Act setting aside seventy acres
for recreation. In 1845 Manchester bought three parks,
Peel's Park in Salford, and Philips' and Queen's Park in
Manchester. In 1855 Leeds bought Woodhouse Moor.
Rochdale, Stockport, Blackburn and Halifax all obtained
parks in the fifties. This had been made easier by the
clause in the Public Health Act of 1848 which allowed
towns to use the rates for making a park without getting
a special Act of Parliament.

Another sign and result of the change was the campaign for public libraries and museums. There were
libraries connected with the Mechanics' Institutions, and
some millowners like the Ashtons, the Strutts, the Mar-
shalls, and the Gregs, had established libraries for their
workpeople in early days. In the forties the practice
spread, and there are several references in the *Leeds
Intelligencer* and other papers to mills that provided
libraries and playgrounds. Peter Ainsworth and John
Bright had libraries for their workpeople. But there
were no public free libraries when Ewart, who occupies
in this crusade the place of honour that Brougham holds
in the crusade for adult education, began his campaign
in 1845. He proposed (March 6) that town councils
should be allowed to impose a rate to establish museums
of art, and he pointed out that with railway transport

it would be easy to send casts from town to town. The debate showed how much this kind of provision was needed, and how strong were the obstacles. The fear of allowing towns to spend public money was so strong that the Bill was only allowed to pass when its operation had been limited to towns with 10,000 inhabitants. The rate sanctioned was a halfpenny, and the charge for admission was not to be more than a penny. The demand that museums should be opened on Sundays was rejected. In 1850 Ewart introduced a Bill to enable town councils to establish libraries and museums. He proposed to abolish the restriction of the Act to towns with 10,000 inhabitants, and to make admission free. There was strong opposition on the ground of extravagance, led by Sibthorp. Ewart stated that Warrington had established a library under the Act of 1845, and that there had been public meetings in Sheffield and Birmingham to demand the Bill. Brotherton, Bright, and W. J. Fox supported him, and in the division Cobden, Hume, and Sir George Grey voted for the Bill, Disraeli and Lord John Manners voting against. In the end Ewart had to accept a compromise, by which the Act was not to be adopted by any town, unless two-thirds of the ratepayers had given their consent.

These were serious handicaps but the movement spread. Warrington opened a public library in 1848; Salford in 1849; Manchester in 1852; Bolton and Liverpool in 1853; Sheffield, St. Helens, Birkenhead, and Preston before 1860. In Manchester a committee of working men was formed to collect a fund for buying books, and £800 was raised by 20,000 subscribers of the working classes for this object, the total sum subscribed being over £10,000.

The change is seen also in the religious life of the time.

"There is no Church, and never was there one," said Landor, " in which the Ministers of religion have so little intercourse with the people as the English. Sunday is the only day that brings them together and not in contact. No feelings are interchanged, or sorrows or joys or hopes communicated. Unpreceded by inquiry or advice, command and denunciation follow the roll call of the day." So Landor wrote in 1836. The Church was still very defective as a moral force to combat the barbarism of the times in the late forties, but there had been a great improvement. Maurice and Kingsley were creating a new conscience in the Christian Socialist movement. Parsons were taking part in movements for reform like the Ten Hours agitation. If Hook was urging Leeds to buy Woodhouse Moor, Prince Lee, the new Bishop, was pressing for a Free Library in Manchester.

In 1850 Convocation of Canterbury passed a resolution recommending that clergymen should live together in poor districts, "preaching, exhorting, visiting the sick and poor in their own homes, and superintending schools." *The Times*, then in the full ardour of the campaign against ecclesiastical abuses of which Trollope gives a picture in the *Warden*, observed on this scheme, "Nothing could be more reasonable than these remarks nor have we anything to add except that in reading them we appear to be reading the description of a collegiate or cathedral establishment engaged in its proper duties."

In the Nonconformist world, too, the failure of religion to meet the needs of the poorest classes had come to be recognized. The rich Methodists of Manchester built a chapel in the slums of Ancoats, the famous Unitarian minister, J. H. Thom, founded the Domestic Mission in Liverpool, and the Methodist Conference published Jobson's book pressing for a different spirit in chapel life.

If we study the local history of the new towns, we find that private benefactions for public amenities become much more common in the forties and fifties. One of the first was Joseph Strutt's gift of the Arboretum to De'by at the cost of £10,000. This was one result of the movement for public parks and libraries. In this respect a change came over social life. One reason for the melancholy condition of the English town was the tradition of private luxury which had become so powerful in the eighteenth century. Bishop Berkeley, writing in 1721, had dwelt on the strong contrast between ancient Greece and eighteenth-century England in this respect. Private splendour was as much a mark of the early industrial age as public meanness; the elegance of the great house as the gloom of the new town. The great house symbolized the pride the great lord took in his place in the national life. The mansion, with its libraries, galleries, parks, reflected the atmosphere of authority, of history, of taste and manners, of a life active, spacious, and delightful. A German observer noticed that Englishmen made more of their country house than of their town house. Now this attractive country life, with its beauty, culture, pleasure, and state, was open to all who made their way into the aristocracy; to the men whom success in business, their own or their fathers', brought into this world. The governing class drew into its orbit almost all those who acquired wealth, setting the standard, mode and plan of life. Hence the uninvested wealth of the Industrial Revolution was largely used for creating new territorial families with mansions and estates in the country. The movement for parks and libraries first taught the English manufacturer and merchant to use their wealth in the spirit of the rich citizens of the Roman Empire.

We get some idea of the difference that the new amenities made if we turn to the evidence given before the
Committee on Public-Houses in 1853. A Rational
Recreation Association had been started at Leeds; popular
concerts were given at the Town Hall, and the Botanical
Gardens had now been thrown open on Sundays. Drunkenness had decreased and manners improved. At Manchester the parks were crowded on Sundays, and the
Zoological Gardens were well attended by persons who
before had spent Sunday dog-fighting or playing at pitch-
and-toss in the beerhouses. At Liverpool, steamers took
crowds across the river on Sundays, and Sunday had
become less drunken. The Committee, reporting on such
evidence, remarked: " Your committee cannot conclude
this portion of their Report without calling attention to
the fact of how few places of rational enjoyment are open
to the great mass of the population on Sunday, which
serve as a counter attraction to the public-house. They
have it in evidence that wherever such opportunities have
been provided, they have been eagerly seized upon, and
have led to the decrease of intemperance."

A chapter of local history given to the first Conference
of the National Association for the Promotion of Social
Science in 1857 showed what could be done by such improvements to draw one of the new industrial towns out
of its morass. A speaker who had taken an active part
in public work at Macclesfield explained that in the year
1847-48 the death-rate in that town was forty-two per
thousand, and that one undrained district of seven streets
was responsible for this high rate, as well as for the crime
of the town. The Public Health Act was adopted and
this district was cleansed and reformed, with the result
that the death-rate had fallen to twenty-six per thousand.
These improvements were followed by others. Baths

and wash-houses were installed, and a public park bought
in which as many as forty cricket matches were sometimes
played on a single Saturday afternoon when the mills
closed. This park was filled every evening in the summer.
The opening of the park had been followed by a remarkable decrease of crime.

Wordsworth, describing mediæval society, made towns
the nurseries of civilized custom:

> " Around those Churches, gathered Towns
> Safe from the feudal Castle's haughty frowns;
> Peaceful abodes, where Justice might uphold
> Her scales with even hand, and culture mould
> The heart to pity."

As he looked at the life of his own age, he gave the
town a very different character:

> " there indeed
> Love cannot be nor does it thrive with ease
> Among the close and overcrowded haunts
> Of cities, where the human heart is sick
> And the eye feeds it not and cannot feed."

Culture was taught to mould the heart to pity, and
light and happiness were brought into the disconsolate
life of these overcrowded haunts by the efforts of men
and women, such as this citizen of Macclesfield, whose
influence on their civilization was as important as that
of the statesmen who struggled over the Corn Laws. But
in comparison they are as little known to fame as the
monk whose patient labour saved for the world the
Histories of Tacitus.

CHAPTER IX

CONCLUSION

THE active city life, described by Mrs. Green in her picture of fifteenth-century England, had sunk into decay long before the steam engine was invented. The ritual of pageants, festivals,. and dances fell into disuse as the cities lost their prestige with the growing power of the Tudor State, and the common people lost their share in the Guilds with the growing power of the richer classes. The towns so proud of their independence had come under the grasp, first of kings, then of families and politicians. The life of ceremony had not disappeared all at once. Leeds commemorated the Peace of Utrecht in 1713 with a great procession and festival. Preston has preserved her Guild Festival to our own day. But it is perhaps significant of the change in city life that the wool-combers' festival in honour of St. Blaise, kept as a popular pageant down to 1825, was replaced by dances and dinners at which the respectable classes entertained each other. The loss of political importance was not, of course, peculiar to the English towns, but Continental towns, though they no longer held the commanding position they had gained in the Middle Ages, had kept much more of the spirit of their rich and interesting past, and its afterglow still comforted and inspired their city life. When the Industrial Revolution collected large populations in the North and the Midlands, the genius of this common life was almost extinct, and a new society had to create its own institutions.

The spirit and manner in which this task was first attempted reflect the ideas and experience of the class that provided the leaders of thought and fashion in the new towns. The pioneers of commerce and industry, who had been gaining wealth and position with such steady progress in the last two centuries, had acquired from their experience definite habits of mind and character. The great commercial and industrial expansion of the seventeenth and eighteenth centuries was due largely to the energy of Nonconformists, who had been excluded or discouraged from a public career by the nature and sincerity of their religious opinions. The pioneers who laid the foundations of the great metal industries were often men who had suffered themselves, or whose fathers had suffered, under Acts of Uniformity and other intolerant laws. Unincorporated towns like Manchester and Birmingham offered a refuge to the uncompromising Dissenter whose conscience would make no terms with Church and State. The vigour and initiative on which the new towns depended were largely to be found in men brought up in this atmosphere, in men, that is, who had been compelled by their circumstances to concentrate their attention on one side of life.

And that side of life had provided them with all that they wanted in the way of romance and adventure. Toynbee describes in his Study of History the effect of a social handicap in stimulating the energies of men who suffer for their opinions. The leaders of town life found in their industrial and commercial enterprises ample field for courage, abstinence and self-command. They looked on their poorer fellows as potential pioneers, able to find and enjoy the same experience. So they came to think that a society of men seeking to get on, thinking always of getting on, sacrificing everything to getting on, would be a happy and stable society.

The virtues on which this view insisted have a special value in times of excitement and change. It is not perhaps surprising that they seemed to make up the whole of good citizenship to men living close to the England that Hogarth painted. There was still a good deal of that England left in spite of Wesley's heroic exertions. But in concentrating on these virtues the rulers of this society put on one side pursuits and enjoy- ments that have interested man at different times of his history and helped to develop his taste, his imagination and his character. Beauty was given no place in work or play, in culture or religion. Nobody can read the description of Coventry in the fifteenth century with its full life of festival and play, given by Conrad Gill in his Studies in Midland History, and then turn to Faucher's description of Manchester without seeing how complete was the breach between the city life of that time and the city life of the industrial revolution.

Mill, criticizing this social life, contrasted it as Arnold had done with the life of the Continent and said that the British insensibility to art as a social influence was one reason why England and the Continent could not under- stand each other. He traced it to three sources; the money-getting spirit which regarded as a loss of time everything that did not conduce directly to its own end; religious Puritanism which looked on feeling as a snare; and the imperfect and misleading psychology of Bentham which, in its simplifying analysis of human motives, left out of account the love of beauty. The first two influences had chiefly shaped the British character since Stuart times; the third was the most powerful influence on the mind of the age.

No educated man will question the immense benefits that Bentham conferred on the English people. Lord Acton, speaking of the intuition that started him on the task of disentangling the injustices of the law, said that " the day on which that gleam lighted up the clear hard mind of Jeremy Bentham is memorable in the political calendar beyond the entire administration of many statesmen." Mill said of him that he found the philosophy of law a chaos, and left it a science, and that he held an indisputable place among the intellectual benefactors of mankind. But it happens that those deficiencies on which Mill dwelt in his description have a close bearing on the social life of the new towns.

For his misleading view of human nature led Bentham to construct a world which Mill described as a collection of persons each pursuing his separate interest or pleasure, in which the law, religion, and public opinion, imposing their several sanctions, serve to prevent more jostling than is unavoidable.

This conception, limited enough in its original form, was not likely to become less limited in the hands of the men who applied it to the new settlements calling for guidance and leadership. The energetic man of business, when told that the best way for him to help the poor of Manchester and Leeds was to make haste to get richer, was not likely to ask himself whether so simple and encouraging a gospel contained the whole truth about something so complicated as a human society, to throw his mind back over history, to recall what had been said on such subjects by Plato or Cicero or St. Augustine or Shakespeare. Nor did it get any less limited in the hands of leaders of morals and manners, who thought that a workman spending a quiet Sunday morning in the public park when he ought to be in a chapel in a black coat was a spectacle so offensive to God that it would bring down on the nation the Divine displeasure.

This philosophy, applied to industry and social life, provoked two agitations, an agitation in the world of literature and an agitation in the world of politics. All that Bentham had forgotten crowded into the pages of Shelley and Wordsworth, Coleridge and Southey, Carlyle and Dickens, Mill and Maurice, Peacock and Disraeli: pages gentle or stern, lucid or confused, pensive or ironical, playing with fancies or thundering with passion. To understand why the Chartist was a figure in history more complex than a man demanding a higher wage, or resenting a particular grievance, we must remember how deeply men and women may be stirred by emotions which they can neither describe nor interpret. The incoherent anger of Manchester and Leeds reflected what those writers had discerned, however unsuccessful they might be in devising remedies: the sickness of a society in which essential instincts were left unsatisfied. The ordinary man would not have put his case as it was put by Wordsworth, or Maurice, or Carlyle, but the error in the ruling philosophy of the time that provoked those writers was the injustice in life that provoked those rebels. Men and women knew that they were the victims of wrong, and that something was false in their world.

The experiment now tried in Manchester and Leeds was not, of course, new in history. The Roman Republic had its great age of acquisition. Dr. Heitland shows in *Agricola* how the early form of domestic slavery changed under the stimulus of the opportunities brought by war and conquest into the hideous system which still dominates our imagination. The crude gospel of gain, pursued without regard to humanity or the welfare of the State, set up the slavery of plantation and mine. The elder Cato, the stern Puritan, the expert in scientific management, told the farmer to sell off his slaves when they grew old with his old iron, and to remember that when a slave was not sleeping he ought to be working. This gospel, pushed ruthlessly in politics, in war, in government, and in industry, nearly brought Roman civilization to an end. The Italian war, the slave war, the civil wars were the penalties paid by the Roman people for that error.

The Roman Empire rescued the world from this disorder. Its spirit is foreshadowed or reflected in the works of a line of great writers. Cicero composed his sermon describing the universal calamities that had followed the worship of wealth and wilful power: Virgil and Horace made contempt for money the characteristic of the true Roman. In these pages we find moralists and poets looking at their age and its evils and perils as Wordsworth and Carlyle looked at the evils of the new industrial age. " Love of men cannot be bought by cash payments," said Carlyle, " and without love men cannot endure to be together." Horace, who had seen a world in which soldiers and politicians gained their power by creating mercenary armies or a mercenary electorate, had drawn the same moral from the catastrophe which so nearly extinguished the Roman genius for government.

> " Can you wonder, when you put money above all else, that nobody pays you the love you do not earn? "— *Sat.*, I. i. 86.

Horace saw, too, that in a society which treated wealth as the measure of a man's worth, discontent was inevitable.

> " But a good many people, misled by blind desire, say,
> ' You cannot have enough for you get your status from
> what you have.' What can you do to a man who talks
> thus? Bid him be miserable, since that is his whim."—
> *Sat.*, I. i. 61.

You may pass Lucullus to-day, but Crassus will be richer
than you to-morrow. Where is it to end?

If we want to find the new spirit at its best, we see it
in the criticisms passed on Cato by Plutarch. " For my
part I look upon it as a sign of a mean and ungenerous
disposition to use servants like beasts of burden and to
turn them off or sell them in old age; as if there were no
communication to be maintained between man and man
any more than interest or necessity required." In this
sentence Plutarch put his finger on the central problem.
The Roman Empire succeeded in controlling and com-
posing the rivalries of men, races, and classes, that had
threatened to destroy civilization, by creating a new
order, inspired by the Greek tradition, aided, as we can
see from Tarn's pages, by the Hellenistic religions which
flourished and expanded when the Greek genius had
ceased to express itself in great literature. For the municipal civilization which spread over the Empire brought
back the amenities and the sympathies on which a Greek
community relied. The basis of this new social life was
the Greek city, with its rejection of the view that a society
is a collection of men pursuing separate interests, ani-
mated by selfish motives, and kept from discord only by
law and other sanctions; and its use of common enjoyments to create and foster the kind of communication
between man and man that makes a stable State.

We are thus brought back to the comparison with
which we started. In all ages the service of man's needs
has occupied great numbers of men and women in hard,
distasteful, and monotonous toil. The ancient world

offered one consolation for that toil, the world of
the Industrial Revolution another. The ancient world
sought to make that lot tolerable by the play of life and
laughter and beauty in its cities. The poor man, sharing
the delight of admiration and the comforts of fellowship,
could imagine, for the hour he passed beneath some noble
portico, or on the ringing benches of circus or theatre,
that drudgery was only part of his life; for when the city
gave its mind to religion or festival, he stood beside his
neighbour, a man among men, lost like his fellows in con-
templation or enjoyment. The new age offered the prizes
of wealth and rank to those who excelled in that toil, but
it treated delights, that had once made the hardships of
common life less rigid and monotonous, as the rewards
of rare success. The arts, instead of helping the com-
plaining and miserable to forget themselves and their
wrongs, were employed to give a new lustre to good
fortune, to declare the glory of sudden wealth. Leisure
was the exclusive privilege of those for whom work was
interesting, giving to those engaged in it a bracing sense
of power.

Now ancient civilization, at its best, was disfigured by
injustices that would have outraged the conscience of the
age of Bentham, and by cruelties that would have revolted
its sense of pity. The critic of the Roman Empire, as
an experiment in making a stable and contented society,
might have pointed to Christianity and similar religions,
spreading in the great towns the voice of a misery which
was bitterly resented. He might have pointed, too, to
the efforts of philosophers to satisfy their consciences by
a more direct encounter with those facts of poverty and
slavery which civilization sought to mask beneath its
smiling amenities; some explaining them in terms of
science, others denying that such hardship could touch

the soul, others, again, taking the heaviest burdens on their own backs to prove how light such burdens were when carried by men who had learnt the difference between true happiness and false. He could thus have shown that the failures of these efforts were as striking as their successes. Yet there was a truth behind those efforts that this new age, rich as it was in knowledge where ancient civilization was ignorant, had still to grasp.

It is obvious that for the majority of human beings a great part of life is occupied with the hard struggle for material security, or material success. The rulers of Manchester or Leeds believed that man could find his happiness in that struggle, clothing it with ambition or piety, giving the look of romance to its dramatic episodes, and making success or failure in that struggle the mark of success or failure in the whole art of life. They held that you could treat the desire to grow rich as the object of universal ambition, and that if the path to its attainment was thrown open, the poor man plodding at his tedious task might dream of his future with all the happiness that Fielding attributed to the young barrister dreaming of the woolsack. Such a plan of life assumed that this struggle called out all man's faculties; that it symbolized somehow the whole of his history, and that it left unemployed and unsatisfied no important element in his nature.

No man can reflect on his own experience without seeing that there is a kind of happiness which is outside that struggle. The happiness that comes to a man when he follows a great play or listens to great music, when he stands beneath a noble building or looks out over a golden landscape, bears no relation to his own ambitions or his own success. The Greeks who could enjoy the plays of Æschylus and Euripides had been taught to look

on the drama as part of their religious experience, lifting
the curtain from ideas too large for daily life. Bradley
makes a comment on Wordsworth and Hegel in his Essay
on English Poetry ("A Miscellany") which helps to
illustrate the argument of these pages. He says of their
philosophy that "the mind of man is no property of his;
indeed, we might say, his private share in it consists of
its limitations, while its greatness is all derived." In this
sense the arts, like religion, enable a man to escape from
his limitations into the peace and beauty that belong to
a universal mind; to re-enter the life of a world that lived
before him and will live after him. The man who can
never so escape is like the man described by Lucretius
(III, 1060), who dashes from his home to the country, and
from the country to his home, restless and weary, a sick
man who knows not the cause of his complaint.

To make a society out of men who are sick is to make
a sick society. Between the spirit of Athens and that of a
goldfield, between a number of persons whose bond of
union is their enjoyment of art, religion, beauty, and
amusement, and the same number of persons whose bond
of union is that each of them hopes to become a rich man,
there is a difference that affects the depths and not merely
the surface of social life. Man who started on his upward
path led by wonder, learning from nature, blending toil
with ceremony, with religion, with dance and play, cannot
be shut inside the narrow circle devised by the old
economists without mortal strain. That is why, when
society is sick from this cause, humanists, who are concerned for man's spiritual interest, have attacked, not
merely the abuses of their age, but its fundamental
philosophy. That is why Cicero, looking at Rome's age
of plunder, said that the worst of all constitutions was
that in which the richest men were counted the best.

That is why Mill, looking at the age of the Industrial Revolution, declared that "the best state for human nature is that in which, while no one is poor, no one desires to be richer, nor has any reason to fear being thrust back, by the efforts of others to push themselves forward."

For the humanists saw that the progress of man has been due to his capacity for disinterested enjoyment and generous pleasure, and that he has succeeded in making societies, just because he could find some other bond between men than the bonds understood by Cato. The pursuit of knowledge and ideas, the search for beauty and feeling in culture and religion, the emotions of pride and pity excited by a common literature and history, these have spread the deeper spirit of fellowship. The ties which unite societies, crossing the barriers of class, of race, and of time, are created by the sympathies that have civilized the habits and the mind of man. "So that if the invention of the ship," wrote Bacon, in a famous passage, "was thought so noble, which carrieth riches and commodities from place to place, and consociateth the most remote regions in participation of their fruits, how much more are letters to be magnified, which as ships pass through the vast seas of time, and make ages so distant to participate of the wisdom, illuminations, and inventions, the one of the other?"

Bridges, describing the birth of man's mind from his response to the beauty of nature, drew a picture of the wolf hunting all his life after nightfall, under starlit skies, without the first inklings of wonder. Yet even the wolf, as he steals across the silence of Mount Olympus, may turn to gaze on the vast peace that lies over the enchanted world described in *Endymion*, the world of bird and beast, of sea and mountain, sleeping in the silver

moonlight. The men and women who now lived in blind
streets had lived, themselves or their fathers, beneath the
open spaces of heaven. In the high moments of his
history man has answered the beauty of nature with the
beauty of cities, but for these exiles the dreams of mind
and hand were as faint and distant as the mountains and
the forests whence those dreams had come. No public
grace adorned·their towns; religion was too often a stern
and selfish fantasy; music and painting were strangers, at
home among the elegant rich, but doubtful of their welcome in this raw confusion; ships brought the riches of
the East across the Indian Ocean, but those other ships
which " pass through the vast seas of time " never spread
their splendid sails. Science herself, the goddess of the
age, kept her gifts for the fortunate. For though man's
power and knowledge had made a new world since
Odysseus fretted for his home in Calypso's cavern, the
spinner, guiding the myriad wheels that clothed the
distant East, was condemned to spend his life longing,
like Homer's ploughman, for the hour of sunset and
supper. But the spirit of wonder which had created art
and religion, music and letters, gardens and playing
fields, still lingered in the toiling men and women who
were shut within these sullen streets. That spirit could
not live at peace in treadmill cities where the daylight
never broke upon the beauty and the wisdom of the
world.

The Age of the Chartists contains, besides the chapters out of which this book has been made, chapters dealing in detail with the government of the new town, the new Poor Law, the state of the towns, the loss of playgrounds, drink, the battle for public health, the Established Church, and the Nonconformist Churches, and the agitations for the Ten Hours Bill and for the Repeal of the Corn Laws.

BOOKS FOR FURTHER READING

R. H. Barrow. *Slavery in the Roman Empire.*
E. Bevan. *House of Seleucus.*
Samuel Dill. *Roman Society from Nero to Marcus Aurelius.*
—— *Roman Society in the last Century of the Western Empire.*
—— *Roman Society in Gaul in the Merovingian Age.*
Gilbert Murray. *The Five Stages of Greek Religion.*
M. Rostovtzeff. *Social and Economic History of the Roman Empire.*
W. E. Heitland. *Agricola.*
J. S. Reid. *The Municipalities of the Roman Empire.*
W. W. Tarn. *Hellenistic Civilization.*
A. E. Zimmern. *The Greek Commonwealth.*
A. M. Duff. *Freedmen in the Early Roman Empire.*
A. J. Toynbee. *Study of History.*
F. von Raumer. *England in 1835.*
Léon Faucher. *Etudes sur l'Angleterre.*
—— *Manchester in 1844.*
A. Redford. *Labour Migration in England, 1800-1850.*
W. J. Warner. *The Wesleyan Movement and the Industrial Revolution.*
J. E. Rattenbury. *Wesley's Legacy to the World.*
R. H. Tawney. *Religion and the Rise of Capitalism.*
Mark Hovell. *The Chartist Movement.*
Julius West. *A History of the Chartist Movement.*
E. Dolléans. *Le Chartisme.*
E. Halévy. *England in 1815* and following volumes.
J. S. Mill. *Autobiography.*
—— *Dissertations.* Vol. I (*Essays on Bentham and Coleridge*).
J. H. Newman. *Idea of a University.*
Graham Wallas. *The Great Society.*
—— *Our Social Heritage.*
Charles Gore. *Christ and Society.*

INDEX

144

Printed by BISHOP & SÓNS, LTD., *Edinburgh*